HURRAH FOR GIN:
RELUCTANT ADULT

Also by Katie Kirby

Hurrah for Gin
The Daily Struggles of Archie Adams

HURRAH FOR GIN: RELUCTANT ADULT

KATIE KIRBY

CORONET

First published in Great Britain in 2019 by Coronet
An Imprint of Hodder & Stoughton
An Hachette UK company

5

A CIP catalogue record for this title is
available from the British Library

Hardback ISBN 9781473662056
eBook ISBN 9781473662049

Typeset in Consolas by Hewer Text UK Ltd, Edinburgh
Printed and bound in Great Britain by Clays Ltd, Elcograf S.p.A.

Hodder & Stoughton policy is to use papers that are natural, renewable
and recyclable products and made from wood grown in sustainable
forests. The logging and manufacturing processes are expected to
conform to the environmental regulations of the country of origin.

Hodder & Stoughton Ltd
Carmelite House
50 Victoria Embankment
London EC4Y 0DZ

www.hodder.co.uk

With all my love to Jim, Sasha
and my beautiful boys x

CONTENTS

OVERWHELMINGLY OVERWHELMED

Once there was a girl. The girl couldn't wait to
grow up so that she could make her own decisions.
She wanted to eat sweets for breakfast and go
to bed at midnight, she wanted to play My Little
Ponies all day and see her friends whenever she
liked, she wanted to be in a girl band and dye her
hair pink and she wanted her own swimming pool, a
unicorn and 3 billion pounds in cash. It wasn't
much to ask.

The grown-ups told her that she was silly to want
to grow up because apparently 'being a kid is the
best time of your life'. She thought they were
lying because they had chosen to live boring,
sad, pathetic lives. So she made a promise to
herself. When she was a grown-up she wasn't going
to be boring or sad or pathetic. Instead she was
going to be mad and wild and fun! Life was going
to be a 24/7 party and no one was going to stop
her.

Three decades later the girl woke up one morning and realised that her life wasn't quite what she had envisioned all those years ago. She had just done what everyone else had done – got a job, got a mortgage, got married and had two kids. And although she was very grateful for her life and loved her family immeasurably, she realised that adulthood wasn't quite as great as it had been cracked up to be.

There never seemed to be time to have fun. It was basically just doing mundane stuff all the time. And the mundane stuff never seemed to end; it just went on and on and on.

She was constantly stressed. She was constantly tired. She was constantly struggling to stay afloat.

She had so many things on her to-do lists (note the plural) that she could hardly see the chicken for the chicken nuggets. She didn't even have the brain cells to think of an analogy that made sense.

It seemed that so much was expected of her!

She was meant to pay bills and keep on top of laundry, she was meant to go to the gym and have an interesting hobby like wakeboarding, she was meant to have a car that wasn't full of old apple cores, party bags and Happy Meal boxes, she was

meant to look stylish in an effortless way, she was
meant to have an expensive skincare routine and
look younger than she really was, she was meant to
be funny on social media without looking like she
was trying too hard, she was meant to live life to
the fullest and travel to interesting places and
also have sensible investments and a pension plan.
She was supposed to run long distances for charity,
make banana bread when the bananas went brown and
volunteer for good causes, she was meant to help
out on school field trips and be on the PTA, she
was meant to maintain a successful career between
the hours of 9 a.m. and 3 p.m. whilst also walking
and playing with the dog (who was bonkers). She
was meant to care about the planet and recycle
and go plastic free and sponsor orang-utans, she
was supposed to know all about politics and be an
interesting conversationalist at dinner parties,
she was supposed to be fun and go out dancing and
also be mature enough to say no to tequila and
not end up puking in the taxi on the way home,
she was meant to refrain from drinking during the
week and find Dry January easy, she was supposed
to enjoy playing with her children and be a nice
calm parent who didn't scream 'JUST GET YOUR BLOODY
SHOES ON!!!!' at them every morning before school.
She was supposed to like watching *Newsnight* and
doing difficult crosswords, she was supposed to
have watched 20 billion episodes of all the most

popular Netflix series because that was all anyone talked about any more, she was supposed to support independent businesses and not just buy everything with one click on Amazon Prime, she was meant to eat free range and organic, she was meant to get her nails shellacked more than once every three years, she was meant to remember to charge her phone and reply to text messages and emails and WhatsApps, she was meant to try and not say FUCK so much, she was meant to try and give up meat and preferably go vegan because she loved animals . . . But the problem was that sometimes the world seemed too bleak and boring and full of admin and just doing the same old shit day in, day out, that she just thought – could I really do this without Camembert and Brie? COULD I REALLY BE EXPECTED TO DO ALL OF THIS WITHOUT BACON?!?!

The answer was no.

Sorry, pigs.

And then one day (even with the bacon) it all became too, too much. So she clicked her slippers together (which were actual slippers and not pointy spangly red things like Dorothy wore because she hasn't been able to walk in heels since 2004) and she said, 'No way! I am drowning here and I cannot do this!'

7

When she finally fell asleep that night (which was at 4 a.m. because she was also an anxiety-ridden insomniac) a fairy godmother came to her in her dreams.

The fairy was wise and told her, 'You may not want to be an adult but you can't go back to being a child again, and even if you could, you wouldn't like it. Things have changed so much . . . they made My Little Ponies into Equestria Girls, which is like some sort of hideous human/horse hybrid thing. It's wrong on so many levels. But listen, I digress . . . you're beating yourself up too much! No one is perfect and no one is getting everything right, it is humanly impossible! Everyone is just trying the best they can and doing two or three of the things on your list - that's it!'

And the girl said to the fairy, 'What, so if I clear out the Happy Meal boxes from the car, bake some banana bread and sponsor an orang-utan then all my problems will be solved?'

The fairy grew impatient with the girl and said, 'STOP BEING SO PEDANTIC!'

The girl apologised. 'I'm sorry, fairy. I know you're right, it's just that when I look at Instagram it seems like everyone else is coping so well - they all have well-behaved, stylish children, go on amazing holidays and have fabulous houses with fancy velvet accent chairs and—'

The fairy was really starting to lose her patience now.

'Instagram is a big bag of shite, you stupid woman! Name me one person in real life who is holding everything together.'

'Errr . . . Helen from number 37?'

'Helen is having an affair with her boss, she drinks fourteen cups of coffee a day, she screams at her children every single morning before school, she has Botox AND fillers, she only pretends to go to the gym, she hasn't vacuumed under the beds for three years and last night she Deliverooed (is that a verb yet because it should be?) KFC for the family dinner!'

'Oh, I didn't know . . .'

'No! You wouldn't know, would you, because you think life revolves around having a fancy velvet accent chair, don't you?'

'Um . . . no . . .'

'Don't lie to me! I saw you – you spent three hours last night looking up velvet accent chairs! Yet still, you complain that you have so much to do, and no time to do it! Have you ever thought that if you didn't waste so much time on your godforsaken phone then perhaps you'd be coping a little better?'

And with that the fairy disappeared in a puff of smoke. Which was a good thing because the girl had started to develop an intense dislike of the fairy because she knew the fairy was right and it was very annoying.

But over the next few days the girl thought about what the fairy had said, and she spent less time lusting over other people's lives on social media and looked about the actual real world. She realised that not everyone was perfect and not everyone was coping and in turn she began to feel much better about her own imperfect, yet sometimes ruddy wonderful, life.

And thus it turned out that an expensive velvet accent chair was not the key to everlasting happiness after all!

THE END.

[Although in the interests of full disclosure, she did in fact buy a fancy velvet accent chair anyway, because although it cost the same amount as a small horse, it really did look bloody good on Instagram.]

YOU CANNOT MAKE
EVERYBODY HAPPY

YOU ARE NOT A PLATE OF
IKEA MEATBALLS

WHY POSITIVITY CAN PISS RIGHT OFF

I have often wondered how some people seem to stay so overwhelmingly positive all of the time. How is it they jump out of bed exuding happiness through their shiny, shiny happy beaming faces?! Are they all on a shit tonne of Valium or is there something wrong with me?

On the face of things – one may argue – it's nice to say nice things and look on the bright side, isn't it? But being nice and looking on the bright side 24/7 (especially in the mornings) can make certain people (me) feel quite ill.

For example, this morning I went to make myself a coffee and found we had run out of milk and it has pretty much ruined my entire day.

You see, I am not one of those glass-half-full types; I'm not even sure I'm a glass-half-empty person either. There really needs to be a third option with a much more exciting drink.

What type of person are you?

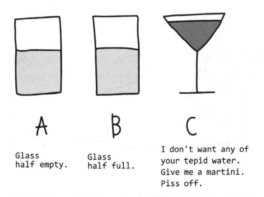

A

Glass
half empty.

B

Glass
half full.

C

I don't want any of
your tepid water.
Give me a martini.
Piss off.

I guess the problem with positivity is that it often just feels a bit too fluffy and doesn't really allow for the huge range of emotions we go through as human beings. Everything isn't always super and great. Sometimes it's OK to feel a bit blue, and wallowing in your own misery can be very cathartic. Too much 'positive thinking' can actually be very draining.

Sometimes when I'm sitting on the sofa in the evening, trying to enjoy feeling sorry for myself and the state of the world we live in (whilst consuming a five-pack of Creme Eggs) a motivational quote will pop up on my Facebook feed and make me feel rather perplexed indeed . . .

If you share this type of bollocks on social media them I'm afraid my perception of you as a person may have gone down quite considerably. I'm sorry, but I feel you're trying to hijack my Creme Egg pity party and I don't think anyone should have the right to take that away from me.

Here are a few of my problems with motivational quotes:

They are super vague

Your generic and meaningless platitudes are just . . . well . . . generic and meaningless.

The more loosely applicable they are to all people, the more they get shared. What do half of them even mean?! Take this one, for example:

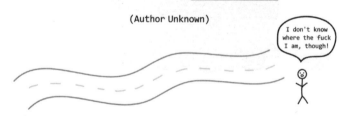

YOU WILL GET THERE
BUT ONLY IF YOU KEEP GOING

(Author Unknown)

> I don't know where the fuck I am, though!

What the hell am I meant to take from that? Of course I will get there if I keep going, unless of course I don't know where I am going and my phone has run out of battery, meaning I'm now without Google Maps and therefore totally fucking lost. I mean, I can remember the way to my Sainsbury's Local easily enough, but with all the will in the world I'm not going to get to Timbuktu, am I?

No. Besides, I have work tomorrow.

Telling people to 'just keep going' when they are headed in the wrong direction is about as useful as a chocolate teapot.

Who even said it?

Of course, there are some exceptionally good quotes out there from the likes of Einstein, Mandela, Gandhi and Dr. Seuss.

Oh, and not forgetting, of course, the people's hero Justin Bieber, who inspires me every day with gems like:

Don't try to be anyone else because that's what makes you not swaggy!

Bow down – nailing it, Justin!

BUT the majority of these so-called 'quotes' aren't actually attributed to anyone with any sort of legitimate authority. Seemingly any halfwit can make one up in minutes by following this simple formula:

1. Pick some nonsensical statement about dreams/ loving yourself/inner beauty/other nauseating tripe.

2. Layer over stock photo of waterfall/mountain range/sunset/purposeful-looking person/all of the above.

3. Stick it on Facebook and go viral.

I could do one right now. See, easy as . . .

Feel free to share!

They are completely without any useful instruction

They make people believe they can do stuff that they can't.

It is all very well telling someone to go and 'make your own sunshine', but how are they meant to actually implement that advice?

I mean, I don't see any recipes on Good Food? Where is Mary Berry's special sunshine recipe?

Convincing people that they are destined for great things when their life is in tatters is counter-productive

Let's look at an example:

Paul has recently been made redundant and is struggling to keep on top of his monthly outgoings. Paul has an auntie called Cheryl, and Cheryl is very worried about Paul's situation – so worried that instead of picking up the phone to talk to him, she tags him in a generic Facebook meme featuring a unicorn.

Paul is immediately inspired! Thanks, Auntie Cheryl! He has always wanted to be a hip-hop artist and now perhaps this is his chance! Should Paul:

A: Move to LA and become a rapper.

OR

B: Call his mortgage company and ask to defer a payment whilst applying for jobs more relevant to his skill set?

It's a no-brainer, right?

Bye, Paul – enjoy your new life!

Now I don't want to ruin the story for you, but unfortunately Paul (aged 42 from Shropshire) wasn't as well received on the hip-hop circuit as he would have liked and thus had to return home and move in with Auntie Cheryl.

Perhaps inspirational quotes should come with their own Ts & Cs.

There is no escaping them!

These quotes are not just confined to social media.
They are everywhere you go. Phone cases, prints,
pencils, mugs, T-shirts and sodding biscuit tins!
If I walk into someone's house and find they have a
huge print of a motivational quote stuck on their
wall I feel I have seriously misjudged them and
want to leave.

For example, this is my worst nightmare:

It is OK to be average

Perhaps most importantly, I must remind you that you do not need to be happy/amazing/grateful/incredible/inspirational 24/7 because that sort of shit is exhausting.

Maybe pick a couple of days a year and try being awesome on those, then the rest of the time, make peace with the fact that being utterly average suits most people just fine.

THE PERILS OF BEING A PEOPLE-PLEASER

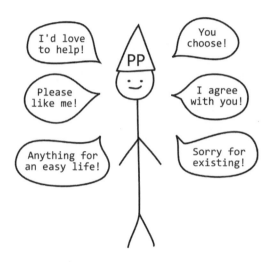

Confession: I am a people-pleaser. I want people to like me. I have a burning desire for people to think I am a nice, funny, kind and decent human being and it is fricking draining.

If you are a people-pleaser too, you may recognise some of the following traits:

People-pleasers can't say no

Imagine this scenario: you are super tired and planning a quiet night in. A friend calls and you make the mistake of answering the phone – it turns out her mate is ill so she has a spare ticket to a gig and she wants you to go with her. There are several reasons why you are not keen on this idea: you are skint, you are already in your pyjama bottoms and favourite bunny-rabbit slippers, the gig is a horrendous death-metal band, yada yada yada . . . In short, you cannot think of anything you would rather do less, and it would be perfectly reasonable for you to say no to your friend.

Go on, try it!

Difficult, isn't it? Because what if your friend has no one else to go with? If you don't go with her she will be very disappointed and you will have caused it! She might never ask you to do anything with her again and you will be marked down as a terrible friend!

Anyway, the upshot is that two hours later you are out of your bunny-rabbit slippers and in the middle of a mosh pit crying. Someone just threw a pint of beer over your head. Or was it piss? Fuck your life.

People-pleasers volunteer for stuff they don't want to do

People-pleasers are so keen to be liked that they offer themselves up for sacrifice by volunteering for all the shit jobs.

When this sort of situation arises, most people avoid eye contact by examining their fingernails, but a people-pleaser's hand starts to rise almost immediately as if it has a will all of its own!

Enjoy judging the contest for the fourth year in a row, muggins! Gary from finance still isn't talking to you after you placed him third in last year's Bakewell tart category!

People-pleasers never complain

I mean, I'm totally fine paying my cleaner £30 to lightly hoover the visible bits of carpet

- how about you? Same with the dodgy meal out or substandard car wash - just chalk it down to experience; anything for an easy life, eh?

This is a people-pleaser ALL OVER. They go to the hairdresser and get a wonky haircut that is nothing like what they requested, but instead of making a fuss they tell the hairdresser they love it. Not only that but they will happily rebook another appointment to avoid upsetting the stylist AND leave a tip.

People-pleasers never ask for help

People-pleasers will help other people in ways that are inconvenient to themselves, but struggle to ask for help when they really need it. If they do actually pluck up the courage to ask for help, they will pepper the question with so many apologies and get-out clauses that it becomes embarrassing for everybody involved.

People-pleasers always try to fit in

Think about this: you're meeting friends in town for lunch and someone mentions a new oyster bar.

They all start talking excitedly about their love of oysters and you don't want to feel left out, do you? No! Best not mention that you can't stand seafood because that would make them all feel awkward, right? Just force them down, girl – that's obviously the best option!

People-pleasers do not like to go against the grain – they will often be so eager to make other people feel comfortable that they will feign interest in stuff they find tedious. The problem is that this can often spiral out of control.

The tsunami of people-pleasing

Imagine that your Uncle Simon is a big fan of birdwatching. Eager to establish some common ground, you listen avidly whilst he talks about his hobby over a family lunch. You ask questions in all the right places and tell him you have always loved birds too (a lie). By the end of the meal you have agreed to go spotting greenfinches with him at the weekend.

Uncle Simon loves that he finally has someone to share his hobby with – everyone else thinks it's boring (he can't imagine why). The next thing you know, he has signed you up as a fully fledged member of the RSPB and convinced you to subscribe to *Birdwatching* magazine.

Then he starts posting pictures on Facebook of the two of you on your birdwatching escapades and now EVERYONE thinks you are super passionate about common garden birds. This is great for your friends and family, who have always considered you difficult to buy gifts for – now they can just get you all kinds of birdwatching paraphernalia without putting any real thought in!

It's starting to get out of hand but you keep quiet, and every Wednesday night you go to a local birdspotters group, drink tea and eat biscuits and talk about the best time of year to spot a mistle thrush and compare photos of various tits' plumage.

Five years later, Christmas Day rolls around again and you open yet another bird-related gift. But try as you might to control your frustration, you have ABSOLUTELY HAD ENOUGH!

This is the fifth year in a row I've got fucking birdwatching binoculars and guess what ... I FUCKING HATE BIRDS! And even if I liked them all I get in my garden is sparrows and they are BORING AS FUCK and I certainly don't need to look at them through FIVE PAIRS OF FUCKING BINOCULARS!

Well done – now you have ruined everyone's Christmas and they all think you are mean and unhinged, and Uncle Simon has locked himself in the bathroom. You could have saved yourself all of this drama by simply saying 'That's cool, but I'm not really into birdwatching myself' half a decade ago.

Perhaps this example is *slightly* extreme, but the message is there all the same: people-pleasers continuously put other people first. They are constantly doing things they don't want to do and staying for longer than they would like for fear of upsetting anyone. Then when they get home they worry that everyone there hated them anyway.

In some ways, being a people-pleaser is an admirable quality as it often means you are kind and considerate of others. But making sure other people are always happy is often to the detriment of your own happiness. The problem with people-pleasers is that they often spread themselves so thinly that they are barely recognisable as actual people any more.

I taste great on crumpets though!

Utterly Pathetic

Now with 75% less backbone
than the average person!

Here is the thing – it is not possible to be adored by everybody. You are not a baby giraffe.

In order for a people-pleaser to stay in control, they must learn to push back on those around them. This is easier said than done, especially if you mix a people-pleaser with a cheeky bastard.

Cheeky bastards can sniff out people-pleasers from miles away because they are extra super clever. They will start off by asking for a small, reasonable favour, which will then escalate quickly until they are leaning heavily on the people-pleaser, who finds it very difficult to see a way out.

Let's say, for example, you have a neighbour who injured his leg playing badminton. You work in the same direction so offer to give him a lift in whilst his sprain recovers. This adds thirty minutes on to your commute but as it will only be for a week or so, it seems like the neighbourly thing to do.

HOWEVER, three months later you are still giving him lifts! He never offers you petrol money or seems particularly grateful – once he even complained that your car smelled like a badger's arsehole! Also you can't be 100% sure but didn't you see him playing badminton again in the park the other day? The neighbour has become a proper cheeky bastard and this has to stop! Come on, psych yourself up and let's tell him . . .

PP: Hi, CB, I'm sorry but I won't be able to give you lifts to work any more. I'm starting work a bit earlier now so the timings won't work.

CB: Oh that's OK, PP – I don't mind getting in earlier.

PP: Well it might be quite early some days, so maybe you could drive yourself in?

CB: Nah, I sold my car – it seemed like a waste of money and I was worried about all the needless carbon emissions.

PP: Well, the bus would probably suit you best then.

CB: Oh I don't like getting the bus because being around members of the public makes me feel queasy.

PP: OK, well, can't your family help?

CB: My family all hate me.

PP: OK . . . maybe a friend?

CB: You are my only friend. *Starts crying*

PP: Oh gosh, don't cry, CB!

CB: Look, PP, I'm having a really difficult time right now, my leg hurts, my family hate me, I don't have any friends, I sold my car, I applied to go on *MasterChef* and got rejected . . .

PP: I'm so sorry – don't worry, it's fine, I'll keep giving you lifts.

CB: OH THANK YOU, PP, YOU ARE SO AMAZING! Also, could you do my grocery shop for me this weekend as my leg is really ouchy at the moment?

PP: Sure.

The mistake the people-pleaser made in this encounter is they used too many excuses, thus enabling the cheeky bastard to offer up alternative solutions and slowly weaken their resolve. They need to learn to stand their ground! Which brings us to the most important part of this chapter:

How do people-pleasers learn to say no?

Well, to borrow the slogan from the well-known anti-drugs campaign and 1986 *Grange Hill* hit single: 'Just Say No'.

Take a look at the examples below:

There is *no need to elaborate,* especially when dealing with a cheeky bastard.

But how do you know if the request is cheeky or not? When should you say no and when is the person just asking a reasonable favour? This can be a difficult conundrum for people-pleasers, so I have prepared a useful flow chart:

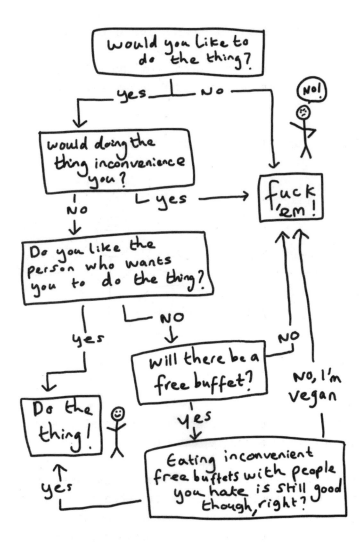

Sounds simple enough, eh?

Let's put it into practice. Imagine the scenario: you are just finishing work for the day, when your colleague Julia gets a call from the vet. Her beloved thirteen-year-old tabby cat Maud has been hit by a car and has died. Julia is devastated; she is sobbing proper tears onto her desk. She is worried about going to the vet alone and wonders if you could escort her there to collect the dearly departed Maud and then wait with her at home until her husband returns.

Whilst Julia is warbling on about Maud all you can think about is the Thai takeaway you are planning to order, the bottle of Prosecco you have chilling in the fridge and the two (yes, two!) episodes of *The Great British Bake Off* you have waiting on your Sky box.

Let's put Julia's scenario through the flow chart.

Would you like to help Julia? No.

Would helping Julia inconvenience you? Yes.
Well . . . Julia does live just round the corner from you, but it's Friday night FFS and the Thai takeaway isn't going to eat itself.

Do you like Julia? Meh. She keeps stealing your stapler and files her nails at her desk.

Is Julia going to provide a buffet? I don't know - ask her?

Sorry, Julia, but the answer is 'fuck 'em'. It's real sad about Maud and all, but she was thirteen and she had a good life.

The downside is that your whole office witnessed this encounter and now thinks you are a cold-hearted bitch, but let's worry about that issue another day because for now Julia's dead cat is not your problem! For now you get to celebrate the fact that you are no longer a people-pleaser. Hooray!

RIP Maud.

HOW TO BE A FUCKING PROFESSIONAL

As we discussed in the first chapter, the common misconception that most kids have, with regard to growing up and becoming an adult, is that it will be really fun and great because you just get to do what you want all the time.

Whenever my kids propose this to me I shut them right down!

I can't wait to be a grown-up and do whatever I like!

WRONG! You have to get a job. There will be bills, performance reviews, tax returns, awkward office parties, the constant threat of redundancy and people cloning your credit card to buy themselves expensive TVs and holidays with YOUR money!

You see, the number one thing that sucks about being an adult is having to have a job. If you don't have a job you can't afford to do anything good and if you do have a job you don't have time to do anything good. It's a lose-lose situation. Unless you're one of the cast of *Made in Chelsea*, who can invite six of your mates to South Africa for three weeks on a whim. Bastards.

Before I had the job of drawing rude sweary stick people on the internet, I had many, many different types of jobs. I wanted to earn my own money ever since I had the capacity to, and that started pretty young. Me, my sisters and a gang of other kids on our street did odd jobs for neighbours such as leaf-collecting and washing cars. We also made horribly sour lemonade and sold it from our front gardens, alongside old toys. Then I had paper rounds and various babysitting gigs and, when I was fourteen, I got my first regular job in the local card shop where I was paid £1.50 an hour. Yes, even taking into account that it was the '90s, that is remarkably crap. I hoovered the shop and restocked the shelves for one and a half hours every day after school, for the princely sum of £2.25. It was shite – but beggars can't be choosers and a beggar I was.

Next, I worked at a bakery where I had to add up the cost of all the goods in my head with a hangover. I worked early shifts in the twenty-four-hour bottle-filling room in the Body Shop factory. I would get up at 4 a.m. every day and come home stinking of Dewberry and White Musk. I worked on the conveyer belt of a hospital kitchen where every once in a while someone would shout 'LIQUID MEAL!' and I'd have to dump a whole roast dinner in a blender. I worked in C&A and got a great discount on Clockhouse – remember that? I worked as a till girl at Safeway and spent all my time obsessing over which of the bag-packing boys I fancied the most. I worked in nursing homes distributing tea and biscuits and listening to the same stories again and again from lovely, lonely old people who never had any visitors. I worked in many bars and clubs, surreptitiously getting drunk for free and joining the party when I clocked off. My best job ever at a bar in Bournemouth continued to pay me for six months after I quit – funding my nights through my final year at university. I couldn't believe my luck.

But still, I couldn't wait to become a proper professional. I didn't want to be the dogsbody skivvy earning a pittance and cleaning the loos

any more. I wanted to be important and go to
meetings in London! I would look at the people
dashing through the streets with nice bags and
lattes, and fantasise about how great it would
be to be so successful that spending £2.80 a
day on a coffee was nothing (even though it all
adds up to over £1k a year!). FYI I used to hate
coffee but, even so, I was so jealous of people
carrying lattes that I trained myself to like it
so I could be part of their 'winning at life'
gang.

Dashing through
the streets with my
massive coffee like
A FUCKING PROFESSIONAL!

I thought my dream had come true when I finished
university and got my first job working in a
fancy digital media agency. It was fun, it was
an experience and ultimately it was also full of

bullshit. Here are a few things that I learned along the way:

Everyone is faking it

On your first day you feel like a total imposter but eventually you realise that no one really has a clue what they're doing and everyone is basically winging their way up the career ladder. (NB This is not applicable to medicine, the emergency services and engineering – I hope.)

Don't panic if you're introduced as someone sounding way above your station. Either nod and agree or, if you can, try and spout some gobbledygook that will impress the other person. Remember – they have no idea what your job involves either, so they will be impressed by almost ANYTHING you say.

Always look busy

The secret to thriving in the workplace is to look incredibly busy and stressed. The advantages of this are twofold: firstly you seem passionate and dedicated, and secondly (and more importantly) people are less likely to give you extra work.

Try some of the tactics below to give the impression you're working really hard, instead of mostly thinking about what you're going to have for lunch.

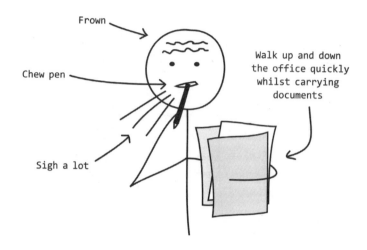

Frown

Chew pen

Sigh a lot

Walk up and down the office quickly whilst carrying documents

Open-plan offices can make it difficult for a work-dodger (or multi-tasker, as I prefer to call it myself). Ideally, seek out a desk that allows you to sit with your back to the wall, and if you can't do that always have a spreadsheet open that you can quickly maximise when your boss walks past. They're unlikely to be impressed if they see that instead of working on an important pitch you are doing a Buzzfeed quiz to find out what type of biscuit you are.

Every once in a while, go to the toilet for twenty minutes, splash water on your face and come back pulling a sad face. People will think you have been crying because you are so overloaded with work. They will have no idea that you are actually feeling great because you just cracked a really tricky level on Candy Crush.

Voluntary overtime

Confusingly, I also learned that in my industry sector, as in many others, you are expected to come in early and/or stay late and work . . . get this . . .

FOR FREE!!! I know.

Even if you don't have extra work to do, you should still aim to work overtime two to three times a week to show how committed you are to the company (regardless of whether or not you give a rat's arse). People will think you'd rather be polishing up an important client report than watching *Location, Location, Location* and that is THE KEY to being a professional. All your colleagues will be doing the same in some sort of misguided game of 'who can stay the latest' chicken. The reality is that you are all simply wasting each other's time.

I'm SO busy! I think I'll be here all night.

Me too! I'm SO busy I might actually die!

Both of these people are actually just buying shit they don't need on Amazon.

Commuting

The traffic was bad, the train was late, the tube was overcrowded, perhaps you walked and you got soaked through by the rain. The opportunities are endless. People LOVE to complain about their commute!

For extra emphasis try carrying a copy of the *Metro* under your arm (or, even better, your respective trade press or the *Financial Times*), then when you get into work, slap it down on your desk in a rather dramatic manner, announcing your arrival.

Looking harassed and pissed off with life is key for any successful person.

NB If your commute was fine, try moaning about the office air conditioning. In my time, I saw fist fights almost break out over whether the air con should be turned on or off.

No smelly food!

During redundancy threats you can bet your bottom dollar that Carol in marketing who heats up her leftover kedgeree will be top of the list. It's not professional, stop it!

Emails

Be very wary of emails. Apart from the odd all-staffer informing you of leftover Pret sandwiches in the third-floor meeting room, they are mostly bad and contain work.

Sometimes it can feel tempting to reply with a curt two-word response; however, being professional means being polite, helpful and accommodating, even when you don't want to be.

Another tactic is to try sending emails out to colleagues and clients at 5.30 a.m. or 11.47 p.m., copying in your boss. This is an excellent passive-aggressive way of reminding them that they are completely fucking up your work/life balance and should give you a pay rise.

Learn how to network

Networking happens at most industry conferences and events and basically is when a load of miserable people are made to stand in a room together for a forty-five-minute window, whilst reluctantly taking each other's business cards. Try to avoid morning networking sessions by hiding in the toilets. Afternoon ones are better as there is usually a bar serving cheap plonk.

If you aren't very good at talking to random people about boring work stuff then try networking with a glass of wine in the corner on your own.

Ace performance reviews

Every once in a while you have what is termed a performance review. You have two aims: to not get fired and to get a pay rise.

Performance reviews are a bit awkward because they usually involve lots of lying.

Boss: Where would you like to be in five years?

Me: Living in a small hut alone in the Maldives far away from all you insufferable arseholes.

Boss: Pardon?

Me: Sorry, I mean I'd like to be here working hard towards a promotion to account director in return for a mediocre pay rise and a shit tonne more work.

Boss: Fabulous!

Another particularly cruel element of performance reviews is peer feedback, in which your boss gathers anonymous comments from your colleagues and presents them back to you in this sort of fashion.

Boss: So one of your colleagues said that although you are a well-liked member of the team, you're not very proactive.

Angrily go back to your desk and try to work out which back-stabbing Judas said that.

Office nights out

Trying to remain professional and well respected in the workplace does not mix well with free, unlimited booze, so approach work socials with caution. Here are a few things I have learned:

1. Jägerbombs are a bad idea.
2. So is loudly slagging off your colleagues.
3. Geoff from accounts is not attractive.
4. No, you probably weren't invited to go clubbing with the graduates.
5. You don't look sexy when you dance.
6. There is no after-party. It's 4 a.m. Go home!

7. Colleagues enjoy nothing more than taking the piss out of you whilst you try to avoid puking in your desk bin the next day.

Going to the toilet

Everybody poos - it's just a normal bodily function. However, you don't want people to know you poo because professional people don't do smelly shits.

You have two options:

1. Hold it in all day and then go straight to the toilet for thirty minutes as soon as you get home (this is what my husband does).

2. Anxiously play a game of toilet roulette and try and spot a gap in between toilet comings and goings in order to make your deposit safely and make a clean getaway.

If you do get caught coming out, you will just have to blame it on the person before you.

Dealing with millennials

Just when you think you have got to the point where you feel secure in your job and are well respected by your peers and valued by your seniors, young, tech-savvy, skateboarding millennials will come in and make you look like shit again.

If you start feeling threatened by their massive headphones, use of acronyms you don't understand and weird food fads, then you are perfectly within your rights to lob staplers at their heads.

I LOVE REALLY MASSIVE KNICKERS

I'm not sure exactly what age it happens, but at some point in your adult life you will go into a clothes shop to have a look around and be horrified. You will suddenly see that it is a loud, terrifying place full of bright lights and teeny tiny items of mouse-sized clothing.

'What's happening?!' you think. 'Have I somehow inadvertently ended up at a rave?'

Shhhh. Don't worry. Everything's going to be fine. It's just Topshop.

Despite your reservations, you start to wander around looking at the 'fashion' and contemplating how on earth you are meant to wear it with love handles, cellulite and a 'mum tum'. The dresses look more like tops and there is literally nothing on sale that you can wear with a bra.

Congratulations – your Topshop days are now over! Please proceed directly to M&S and marvel at how fashionable the clothes are these days. But are they more fashionable, or are you now just a lot less fashionable? Best not to think about that one too deeply.

I mean, I know a lot of people who've moved over to Boden, but I don't think I'm strong enough for that just yet. It is lovely quality, though, so . . .

I'll level with you here: I have never been someone who has really enjoyed shopping. I have never been the type of person who puts on an outfit and then parades around the changing room in front of friends, inviting their opinions. I just don't really like people looking at me that much and if I'm being completely honest, I've never liked looking at my own self in the harsh conditions of a shop changing room, because of two horrible (could we even say malicious?) features:

STRIP LIGHTING

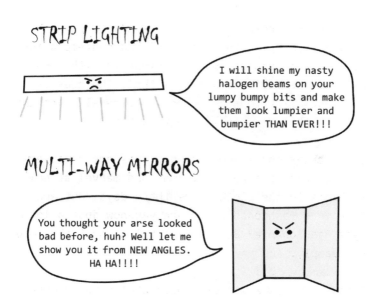

I will shine my nasty halogen beams on your lumpy bumpy bits and make them look lumpier and bumpier THAN EVER!!!

MULTI-WAY MIRRORS

You thought your arse looked bad before, huh? Well let me show you it from NEW ANGLES. HA HA!!!!

I mean, do they even stop to consider if people actually want to see themselves in tiny detail from every angle? To be honest, ignorance is often bliss and I'd just rather not know.

For these reasons, along with a lack of time and dislike of the general public, I buy the vast majority of my clothes via the fabulous mechanism of the internet, which has changed this element of my life massively for the better. Now I can try clothes on in the comfort of my own home and I can turn the lights down as low as I like and peek out from behind my fingers if I so choose.

However, there are a number of items of clothing that are very difficult to shop for online and which require an anxiety-ridden outing to the shops.

One of these items is jeans. Unlike a comfy jumper, jeans are practically impossible to buy online once you hit a certain age or, errr, physique and all of your lumps and bumps have fallen into different places.

I remember back in the day there was only one type that meant anything – boot-cut. I used to wear them long, trailing over high-heeled loafers. Nowadays there are more than 17,236 different species of jeans on the market and scientists are discovering new breeds every day.

There are regular-fit, high-waisted, mid-rise, low-rise, practically-see-your-pants-coming-out-rise, skinny, super-skinny, super-ultra-skinny, cropped, ankle-grazers, cigarette-cut, straight-leg, jeggings, spray-on, relaxed, high-maintenance, distressed, going-through-a-bit-of-a-rocky-patch, and the list goes on . . .

Mum jeans

Boyfriend jeans

Auntie Linda jeans

Your dodgy ex Steve jeans

Awright darlin!

Plus mostly they all have massive holes all over them. I went shopping just the other day to buy myself a pair of new jeans because I had unfortunately bust the knees of my old faithfuls. The only pair I could find that fitted was another pair with massive holes in the knees. I was so overjoyed to find anything at all that I bought them anyway.

When I got home I tried to explain the logic to my husband, even though I couldn't quite understand what I had done myself.

The problem was that it was January and I had to put up with very cold knees for the rest of the winter. I hate it when he's right.

Finding the perfect jeans can sometimes feel like an impossible quest. Only the very hardiest and determined among us make it to the Holy Grail.

If jeans are bad, then underwear is not much better. There are also literally billions (OK, not literally, but lots) of different types of pants and bras. Every time you go to get measured up for a new bra the fitter will take delight in telling you that you are wearing completely the wrong size. There doesn't seem to be any real science behind it and it could change from one day to the next.

It is no wonder we remain devoted to our greying baggy pants and tattered bras until the bitter end. Only when the crotch starts to disintegrate and the underwire threatens to impale us through the heart, do we finally accept that the relationship is over.

You see, much like with jeans, it is practically impossible to find a bra that is comfortable, well fitting and doesn't look like something from the 1950s.

Even walking through a lingerie department can feel daunting as you survey the styles available, already envisioning all the issues they will cause . . .

You may think knickers would be simple, but again there are just too many varieties these days, from a flossy thong to full-on granny pants. And I know which way my cookie crumbles.

On a recent knicker-shopping expedition I became a bit confused by all the names (the bikini, the Brazilian, the low-rise, shorts, the midi and the full brief) so I decided to ask the shop assistant for help. You see these days, I have no time for pants that disappear up my arse.

'I just want to make sure I get the ones that cover my whole bum, please?' I begged.

She looked me up and down and said, 'Hmmm, you aren't old enough for the full brief yet, are you? Maybe try the midis?'

I learned that the midi is quite a good full pant with adequate arse coverage, somewhere between normal knickers and a pair of shorts. I guess a bit like granny-pant training knickers.

I was kind of pleased to be deemed too young for the granny pants, yet also a little upset that I wasn't allowed to have any.

So obviously I shoved some in my basket anyway, because everyone has big pants days now and again and surely one of the best things about getting older, and being in a long-term relationship, is that you no longer have to wear tiny lacy undercrackers to impress anyone! Which means that I am finally WINNING AT LIFE because . . .

MUMMY LOSES THE PLOT

It is Sunday lunchtime at Topsy and Tim's house and Mummy has been making a delicious roast dinner whilst listening to the twins complain about how difficult their lives are.

She is in a happy mood and nothing will break her. Even when Tim pisses all over the toilet floor (again) she cleans it up with a heart full of joy.

Mummy has just finished Febrezing Tim when she hears the key turn in the lock. Oh good – Daddy is home from surfing!

Daddy likes going surfing because he is approaching forty and struggling to come to terms with his pathetic existence. Daddy is the twins' favourite parent, despite the fact that he prefers surfing to spending time with them.

Mummy knows they are joking and that deep down they appreciate everything she does for them.

'OK, everyone, dinner time,' she calls.

Mummy is looking forward to the delicious meal because family time together is very precious. It's lovely to sit down around the table and have a proper conversation . . .

After dinner, the twins carry on being cute and adorable so Mummy makes herself a nice mug of wine and sits down to read the *Sunday Times* style supplement.

Aaaaaaaaand relax . . .

Mummy might sometimes feel tempted to tell Topsy to PISS RIGHT OFF but she is a good person and she knows that children are a blessing so instead she takes everybody to Hobbycraft and spends £137 on glitter glue.

Later on, to thank her for her generosity, Topsy throws Mummy's expensive perfume out of the bedroom window for fun.

It is now 7 p.m., which is the twins' bedtime. Mummy breathes a sigh of relief — she has been so patient and kind all day that we mustn't begrudge her looking forward to getting the children to bed.

Unfortunately, instead of going to bed the twins choose to spend two and a half hours dicking about. When they do finally make their way upstairs there is an exciting revelation . . .

Bollocks.

The twins would love to help Mummy but it is now 9.37 p.m. and they are very tired from all of the dicking about.

Daddy would love to help Mummy too but he is busy finishing off an important work presentation. Instead he pops in every twenty minutes to get another beer and offer some constructive feedback.

I LOVE MY LIFE, thinks Mummy as she attempts to fashion the dome out of Müller Crunch Corner pots.

Mummy finally crawls into bed at 2.37 a.m. She is exhausted but thankful. ALWAYS thankful.

At 3.48 a.m. Tim wakes up in a pool of piss.

At 4.47 a.m. Topsy wakes up because she has been having a nightmare about the whole family getting chopped up by a huge machete-wielding bunny rabbit.

At 5.25 a.m. the twins wake up for the day. Mummy has had approximately eighteen minutes of sleep, which is fine. It's just fine, isn't it?

But she is feeling a wee bit tired, so instead of making them their usual organic goji berry

granola, she gives them the iPad and a packet of
KitKats for breakfast.

It's a one-off, OK!!!!!!!

Mummy carefully carries the Müller Crunch Corner
Taj Mahal to school. She is very tired now and
looks a bit like an extra from *The Walking Dead*.
On the way, they bump into Capable Louise. Capable
Louise has about fifty children, who always look
nice and clean and clean and nice.

Oh dear.

There is a long awkward silence as Mummy processes this information.

She tries to think of something a nice mummy would say but she CANNOT!

SHE IS ALL OUT OF NICE.

She has had enough.

'And that,' said Mummy, 'was that!'

THE END.

THE WORRY SPIRAL

Once, as I was leaving work (way back when), I bumped into my boss and he mentioned he wanted to have a chat first thing in the morning. He didn't say what it was about so I immediately went through all the potential scenarios in my head, largely focusing on the negative. Half an hour later I had decided that I was definitely getting the sack. This was grossly unfair! I had been working really hard lately (or at least pretending to work really hard, as per the 'How to Be a Fucking Professional' chapter). How dare he?!

I spent the evening imagining the meeting, playing out what we'd say to each other, word for word. My heart was beating really fast as I formulated all of my best comebacks and stated my case to my boss like a badass.

Soon it was 3.37 a.m. I was furious, my boss was an utter, utter arsehole and I'd not slept a wink.

The next day I went into work, sleep-deprived and jittery. My boss called me into his office and asked my opinion on venues for the office Christmas party.

I slapped him round the face with a metaphorical fish and told him that he could stick the office Christmas party where the sun don't shine (sadly, this was only in my head).

DAMMIT!!

I'd done it again. Cursed be the overthinker!

This happens to me all the time because . . .

Hello, my name is Katie and my hobbies include eating crisps, reading, fawning over cute animals and over-analysing everything!

The problem is that I have a very thinky brain. Sometimes that's OK – I like daydreaming and remembering lovely things about the past; it makes me happy. Other times it's a bloody nightmare because my thinky brain leads me down a destructive path littered with doubt and anxiety.

I wish I had the type of brain that is able to think and worry to normal levels and not upgrade small things into a nuclear apocalypse (although, to be fair, a nuclear apocalypse is becoming a very real threat these days).

Overthinkers have a natural tendency to strive for perfection; they do not want to do a bad job or make mistakes. They want to be liked and accepted and they do not want to let people down. On the face of it these are good traits, but it's not possible to get things right 100% of the time, and the incessant worrying can become debilitating.

If you are an overthinker, you may worry that your house is burning down because you accidentally left your straighteners on – even though you checked you switched them off three times before you left home. You may worry that Gavin at work doesn't like you (even though you don't really like Gavin) – WHY doesn't he like you?! You're a nice person, goddamn it!

You may worry because your next-door neighbour has your recycling bin and you are too scared to ask for it back because . . . did they steal it or did they just take it by mistake? You worry about the potential fallout from the confrontation you take three days to psych yourself up for, each time imagining it turning into a heated argument . . . only for them to reply with something like 'Oh sorry, mate, thought it was ours!' As simple as that. They hadn't even noticed! But yet again you wasted precious hours of your life worrying about problems that were not even there.

Do you recognise this one? You wake up at 5 a.m. after a lovely night out with old friends, with the panicky feeling that you may have accidentally offended someone or done something stupid.

OH MY GOD, I'M SUCH A DICK!!!

Suddenly you are dissecting entire conversations.
Did Molly take your joke the wrong way? When Liv
and Sonia were chatting in the corner, was it
about you? Did you drink too much? Did you laugh
too loudly? Was your outfit a bit slutty? Were
you too quiet . . . maybe everyone thinks you're
boring? Maybe you talked too much . . . did you
ask everyone questions about themselves? Were you
being self-absorbed – AGAIN! Were you insensitive?
Oh god I bet you were gossiping . . . and being a
bit bitchy! Did they even want to invite you? Were
they just being polite? Do they actually like you?
WHY CAN'T YOU JUST BE NORMAL?!?!

This is how the worry spiral works. You pop a little worry in at the top and get something much worse at the bottom.

The worry spiral

Minor health niggle

Terminal illness

A few weeks ago I developed a sharp, intense pain in my ribs. Fifteen minutes later I had google diagnosed myself with pancreatic cancer and was visualising my friends and family huddled around my deathbed crying and saying goodbye. Then I was looking down on my own funeral: everyone was wearing white, which was odd, and someone had made a nice montage of my best bits like they do on *Big Brother*. It was tasteful, I guess, but the fact was that I didn't want to be dead. Luckily for me it turned out to be indigestion, which was easily corrected by some Gaviscon.

There is no denying that this is a horrible and unhealthy thought process, but the problem is that it is very difficult to stop. Unnecessary worrying can almost seem like a leisure pursuit. It's a little bit like going on a helter-skelter that's not very enjoyable.

Even when you try and say no . . .

It's very difficult to stop yourself getting sucked in . . .

Deep down we all know that overthinking is pointless.

It means you find it really hard to be present because you are either worrying about things that have already happened, which you can't change, or things that haven't happened yet, and probably never will!

It stops you being productive and making decisions. It stops you taking chances and trying new things.

In short, that critical inner voice is just a massive waste of your time and mental energy, and listening to it is only holding you back.

The stages of overthinking

The problem is that like a lot of other overthinkers, I know that I'm overthinking things but I can't do anything about it. Sometimes I even overthink about overthinking. I am able to advise other people on more sensible, rational scenarios but I cannot seem to compute that sort of logic myself.

So how does one access logic in the brain? Let's talk science!

Here is a detailed drawing of an overthinker's brain; in the centre there is a very small spot denoting logic. This can be difficult to get to as it is surrounded by so much irrelevant gobbledygook.

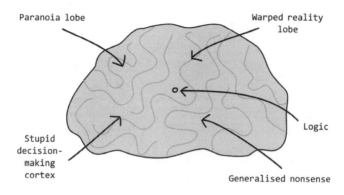

2.1b A scientific diagram of a brain

Paranoia lobe

Warped reality
lobe

Logic

Stupid
decision-
making
cortex

Generalised nonsense

If you ask other people for advice on how to cut
through the nonsense, you will generally get
answers such as 'Have you tried mindfulness?'

In reply I'll normally say something like 'Not
really because I have a very thinky brain and I
really don't think it's possible to switch it
off . . .'

But they'll be all like 'OMG, try this app, it's
changed my life! Honestly I used to be like you
and now I'm super chilled and it's ALL because of
this AMAZING APP on my phone!'

So I'll be like 'Okaaaaaaayyyyyyy . . .' but I've
got nothing to lose so I download the app and give
it a bash.

And I try. I swear I do try!

Breathe in ... breathe out ... imagine you are lying by a waterfall ... imagine the birds are singing ... IMAGINE GETTING MAULED TO DEATH BY A BEAR ... breathe in ... breathe out ...

DAMMIT AGAIN!

P.S. I'm sorry if you were hoping for this chapter to end with some sort of magical solution to overthinking, but it's really not that sort of book. I just wanted you to know that you are not alone with your stupid thinky brain that refuses to calm the fuck down.

P.P.S. Sometimes just saying 'YES!' really quickly helps. You can worry about all the things that could go wrong later, but at least you won't be worrying about the chances you didn't take.

THE DOUBLE CLEANSING FAILURE

It's a horrifying moment when you look in the mirror and for the first time notice that you are starting to look old. I don't just mean a couple of fine lines, I mean actual signs of actual ageing. I remember feeling afraid – what was happening?! I tried to recall the last time I had been ID'd in Tesco and I couldn't. I used to love getting ID'd and pretending to be all embarrassed about it whilst secretly revelling in it.

But not any more! Now I obviously fall into the 'not even a smidgen of any doubt this haggard-looking person is anywhere near worthy of a Challenge 25 check' category. Sad times.

I looked different and I couldn't quite put my finger on why. I mean, there were some wrinkles, but they weren't that bad. I started looking at the faces of younger people when I was out and about, trying to work out exactly what it was that made them look so young, and I came to the startling realisation that it was simply their glowing skin. It was luminous, radiant and bright, they had a whole life of possibilities flowing from their perfect microscopic pores!

In comparison I just looked permanently irritated, blotchy and a bit grey.

I started getting annoyed with people looking at me and saying, 'Are you OK? What's wrong?'

And having to try and resist shouting back, 'NOTHING, THIS IS JUST HOW MY FACE IS NOW!'

I remembered when I was younger, my parents had warned me how quickly life would go; I arrogantly assumed they were talking nonsense and that I would be aged twenty-something forever. Now I realise they were right.

I wanted to run after these glowing youths and warn them of what was coming!

I didn't even used to know saggy eyelids were a thing! I wished I could tell them to appreciate their youthful eyelids whilst they had them, but on reflection I thought that going up to strangers and screaming in their faces about eyelids might make me seem a bit crazy.

So I stayed hiding behind my bush for a bit longer . . .

I guess I'd better leave soon before I get arrested.

Later when I got home I looked at old photos of myself. I used to be just like them, with plump round cheeks. Look at me now, beaten down by the responsibilities of life – struggling to carry my groceries to the car like some sort of modern-day Gollum.

OK, maybe that's a tad exaggerated, but still.

Anyway, this was all very upsetting, but not as upsetting as the time I happened to turn on an episode of *Lorraine* and see her interviewing Natalie Imbruglia, who looked nothing short of amazing. Thinking back to her 'Torn' fame I was like 'Hang on a minute, I thought she was older than me?!' So I googled her and she is! I can hardly bear to even write this down . . .

SHE WAS FORTY FUCKING THREE YEARS OLD!

I wanted to be sick. I already had to deal with younger people looking younger than me, but now

I also had to face the gross injustice of older people looking younger than me too?! Where the hell did she get off looking so incredible?

But I reasoned it was not too late. I just had to be more proactive regarding my skincare regime, and by that I mean actually getting a skincare regime that involved more than just face wipes.

So I started researching, and the more I read the more horrified I became. There was so much to take in – so much advice, so many different routines and products. I just wanted to grab my laptop screen and beg it 'PLEASE, FOR THE LOVE OF GOD – JUST TELL ME WHAT I NEED TO DO?!?!?!'

Life was so much simpler when I was nine years old and all I had to do was occasionally remember to wash my face with a wet flannel.

The thing that I was most alarmed to discover was that I should have been using anti-ageing skincare products since my mid-twenties!

Fuck.

Why did nobody tell me this? Surely there should be some sort of official government advice or something. I mean, Natalie knew! How did Natalie know?!

One article by a dermatologist talked about clueless women who came to her when they were approaching forty, looking for anti-ageing advice – she said when she asked them if they were using retinol the majority of them had never heard of it! Apparently they had missed out on over ten years of its amazing benefits, which were now nigh on impossible to get back. She said she felt really sad for these 'poor women'. I felt really sad for poor me :(

I emailed her and asked if I did shots of retinol and stuck six syringes of Botox in my face, might that make it possible to catch up?

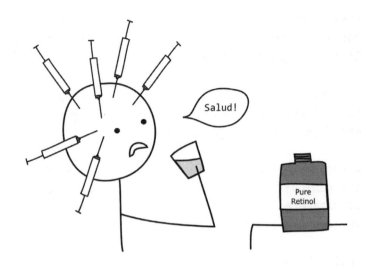

She didn't reply.

I went back to my research. Everything said 'prevention is better than cure'.

FAT LOT OF GOOD THAT WAS TO ME NOW.

The other thing that I learned was that I was doing everything wrong and I was going to have to put a lot more effort in. Rubbish. Firstly I should be 'double cleansing', which basically translates as washing your face twice in a row with a fancy little cloth. I should also be regularly burning the top layer of my skin off with acid, using various types of serum/eye gel/elixir/moisturising

cream, spritzing it with some spritzy face mist and applying concentrated intestines of a baby cow.
It sounded like a lot of work.

Remember this slogan: *'Spend time on shampoo and conditioner? Take two bottles into the shower? Not me! I just want to wash my hair and go!'*

I wanted the skincare equivalent of Wash & Go, but there didn't seem to be a simple one-pot solution. It was more: *'Why use one type of face serum when you can use 218?'*

Again. Rubbish.

Please can someone invent this:

Makes you look
a bit less dead!

97% of people reported
looking slightly like
Natalie Imbruglia after one week

But the worst bit of all was reading that
my trusty face wipes were . . . get ready for
this . . . EVIL! Apparently using them was
committing the ultimate skincare sin, because
they don't clean your face properly AND they can
lead to EXTRA wrinkles AND they are bad for the
environment. Boo.

I plodded on regardless. I just had to accept
that by the time I had worked my way through the
eighty-seven steps of the process, getting ready
for bed would now take approximately two hours.
My husband started getting suspicious. Why was I
spending so much time alone upstairs?!

But he didn't argue much as he fancies Natalie Imbruglia. As do I.

And so, for a while, I kept up with the skincare regime, and it was certainly a regime. And perhaps I did start to look a little bit less dead, but not as good as Natalie Imbruglia. The problem was I just kept thinking about my face wipes and how easy life had been when I just had to wipe my face and hop into bed.

Then one night when I was really tired and I couldn't bear to wash my face and get water in my hair and on my pyjamas, and I couldn't bear to get cleanser in my eyes and apply a million different types of potion, I saw my face wipes winking at me from across the bathroom, and I thought . . . fuck it!

So I plucked one from the packet and I wiped it over my face and it felt SOOOOO good (and a little bit naughty). It took thirty seconds and then I got into bed, the thrill of my dirty deed pulsing through my veins as I fell into a restful sleep.

Little by little I started to use my wipes again. First after a night out when it was late, then just when I couldn't be bothered, then every few days, then every other day and then EVERY DAY!

Like an addict who's failed at rehab, guiltily I looked around to check no one was watching me, half expecting skincare guru Caroline Hirons to jump out of my wardrobe and reprimand me like I was a disobedient schoolgirl.

I didn't want to let Caroline down – I really wanted her to be proud of me. And to be honest I'm sure she has better things to do than hide in the wardrobes of all the people who have tried and failed at double cleansing.

But I wagered that even though my skin may be looking older, it's not so bad. I mean, it's there and it helps keep my insides in! And me and face wipes, we just get each other, you know? Plus you can get biodegradable ones now too – hurrah! So the lessons I've learned are that maybe Natalie Imbruglia is some sort of cyborg or at least very genetically blessed, and that sometimes you just have to listen to your heart and stay true to whichever skincare product you click with the bestest.

#facewipes4eva

THE PERILS OF BEING 'FINE'...

HOW TO HOST A SOPHISTICATED DINNER PARTY

Now most of your friends have kids and all of their money is being spent on childcare, Lego and unsolicited in-app purchases, dinner can be considered a good and inexpensive way to socialise. Long gone are the days when your income afforded you the luxury of eating out three times a week!

It can feel daunting when it is your turn to host but don't worry, here is a handy guide to help you plan the perfect evening:

- Invite a good mix of people. Preferably guests should know and like each other (at least a bit). You are not aiming for a *Made in Chelsea* showcase showdown.
- Devise a menu. Ideally this should be posher than you'd normally eat, so Heinz tinned ravioli is a no-no. Something like chicken in Parma ham is ideal. If you can only cook spag Bol then

that'll have to do – just do some posh sides to make it look like you're trying.

- Do an easy pudding that doesn't involve any cooking. Consider a Viennetta as some sort of ironic nod to your 1980s childhoods.
- Now also provide meat-free, dairy-free and gluten-free alternatives for each course.
- Buy some wine. Don't be too cheap! People *will* be judging you. Everyone will be impressed if you serve Oyster Bay. Jacob's Creek less so.
- Choose your outfit. Why not channel your inner Nigella and go for:

SEXY
POSH
CHEF

- Make sure you clean your toilet. No one wants to see piss all over the floor and your six-year-old's unflushed turd.

- Lay the table. Matching wine glasses please! It may have been OK in your student days, but drinking wine out of a pint glass is now generally considered passé.
- Light some candles. Try not to set fire to the house, though!

- You may be feeling a bit nervous, so it's OK to have a glass of wine before your first guests arrive.
- Maybe two glasses?
- NO. Three is bad. Stop it!
- Put on some background music that everyone hates, such as jazz.
- Shit, they're here! Put some nibbles out for your guests to enjoy as they may be hungry if

coming straight from work. I know everyone likes them but avoid Flamin' Hot Doritos – that is not the vibe you are going for. Bombay mix and stuffed olives suggest you are classy and cultured.

- Errr, Pringles aren't great either . . . but yes, I do understand they are good for party tricks.

Ah, good evening Tom and Rachel!
Have you finished off your utility room renovations yet?
Oh how rude of me, you must be starving ...
Would you like a Pringle? I can use them to do an impression of a duck! QUACK QUACK!

- Time to finish cooking the food. FYI this is not an opportunity for you to get really twatted whilst doing so!

- Serve your delicious meal and continue to ask dull adult-y questions about house prices, tax, planning permission and DIY.
- Try not to kill self with boredom.
- Remember not to drink too much.
- I said remember not to drink too much!
- Don't start going round the table doing a character assassination on each of your guests. It may seem funny at the time but it's really not.
- Don't tell embarrassing stories about everyone . . . like the time Andy shat himself on a night out.
- OK, maybe try and lighten the mood!

- Remember it's not 2002 any more.
- Don't talk about the time Mel had an affair.
- FFS I said *DON'T*.
- Calm the situation by asking if anyone wants cheese and biscuits.
- Plonk a block of cheddar on the table. Tell everyone to pass it round and take a bite as you can't find any crackers or clean knives.

- Suggest gin and tonics as a nightcap.
- Make quadruple G&Ts and serve them in pint glasses.
- Start swaying and/or crying whilst singing 'Eternal Flame' by the Bangles.
- Yes, yes you may as well get up on the table.

- Hear your guests start to murmur, 'I think we'd better call it a night . . .'
- Go to bed in your clothes.
- Wake up and survey the damage.
- Congratulations – now everything is ruined.
- Feel momentarily cheered when you remember you forgot to serve the Viennetta.
- Feel bad again when you remember that you called Andy a cock nose.
- OH GOD!! Visions of assaulting Nina with the block of cheddar!
- Eat the entire Viennetta. Surprisingly enjoyable, aren't they?

- Text everyone to apologise.
- Never have a dinner party again.
- Feel anxious for eternity.

NOTE TO SELF ...

THE SHITTY GUILT FAIRY

I often find that whilst I'm trying to be happy and enjoy life, there's a constant buzzing sound in the background. You may have heard this irritating buzzing too and not realised what it was . . .

Let me introduce you to the Shitty Guilt Fairy. She's kind of like Tinker Bell but WAY uglier and a total bitch. Instead of carrying a wand she carries around a shovel of shit, which she cracks into the back of your head whenever she feels like you're doing a bad job. Which, it transpires, is quite a lot.

Hello, I'm here to make your life suck!!

The purpose of this fairy is to make you feel shitty and guilty about stuff (hence her name).

For example, it can be very difficult to enjoy eating your favourite treats without her making an appearance.

She also likes to remind you of all the things you said you'd do . . . and didn't actually manage.

If you have children then she has an absolute field day!

You shout too much, you make empty threats, you'd rather give them an iPad than re-enact the 'Pups Save a Pool Day' scene from *Paw Patrol* for the 127th time.

She gets her knickers in a right twist if you serve them chicken nuggets for dinner instead of an organic homemade fish pie.

And heaven forbid you try and have a career as well as being a mum!

She sees that you're working hard, she knows you're getting close to breaking point, but she can't help pointing out everything you're doing wrong and all the people you're letting down.

Sometimes she makes you feel like you're failing at everything.

And life can become too, too much.

It only takes one little thing to push you over the edge, one last stinky sock that didn't make its way into the laundry basket, and all the pent-up guilt and feelings of inadequacy can spill out as anger – often directed at the people who care about us the most.

And then you feel a million times worse. It's no wonder in this modern world, where we're constantly bombarded by other people's narratives, lifestyles and achievements, that we can end up feeling like we aren't doing a good enough job.

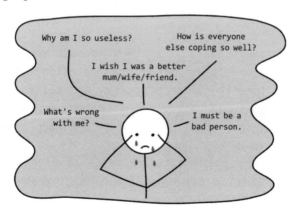

It's no wonder that this sense of failure starts to affect our mental health. And the less we talk to each other, the more likely it is that we develop anxiety and depression.

Yet the Shitty Guilt Fairy wants you to keep plodding on; she doesn't want you to 'burden other people' with your 'pitiful problems'. She makes you feel guilty for asking for help and she makes you feel guilty for taking the medication that enables you to cope.

But let me tell you this.

There is no shame in struggling, there is no shame in finding things hard and there is absolutely no shame in getting the support you need, whenever you need it.

Because nobody is perfect, and nobody is always getting it right — we are all just winging it as best we can.

If we talked more, and compared less, we'd soon see it.

As for guilt, guilt is just a massive waste of time.

And guess what — the Shitty Guilt Fairy HATES being called a waste of time! It makes her feel weak and vulnerable, thereby providing the perfect opportunity to take a big fly-swatter and go at her hard until her wings are mangled to fuck.

Don't feel sorry for her. It's no less than she deserves.

Once she's gone, instead of thinking about all of the things that you're getting wrong, try and think about all of the things you're getting right. No matter how small.

A GUIDE TO SURVIVING SMALL TALK

Imagine a world with no small talk? Imagine a world where it was perfectly acceptable to ignore people unless there was a need for meaningful and enjoyable conversation.

It's hard, isn't it, because according to the Bureau of Made-Up Facts (2018), the average British person discusses the weather approximately 11.7 times per day. It is therefore virtually impossible to bump into an acquaintance and not comment on how hot/chilly/misty/rainy/snowy/pleasant it has been lately.

I'm sure there are some people out there so comfortable in their own skin that they do not need to waste time trying to win over the affections of those they barely know, but sadly most of us are not that confident.

Therefore it is important to master the art of pointless dialogue, and with that in mind I have put together a handy guide that looks at how to equip yourself in several perilous environments where small talk is rife.

Work

First, let's look at one of the most popular areas of small talk – asking about a work colleague's weekend. This is perfectly appropriate small-talk ammo for a Monday, and possibly Tuesday, but you may find yourself desperately clinging to it throughout the week for lack of literally anything else to say.

The downside to weekend-based small talk is that under pressure it can be very difficult for a middle-aged person to recall anything they did at all, because of their rapidly dying brain cells and the fact that they never go out any more unless it's a trip to B&Q or the tip.

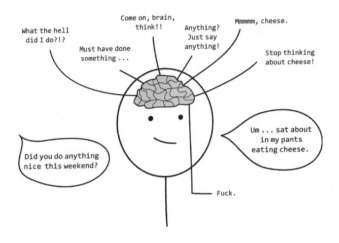

Let's look at some examples of good and bad responses to the question: 'Did you have a nice weekend?'

Example one

I think we can all relate to this guy but his response has several negative connotations:

- It's a bit rude.
- Swearing can be considered offensive, especially words like fuck and the one beginning with 'c' that I won't say as my mum will be upset.
- It's unlikely to make you many friends.

The plus point is that although it might not be considered a very polite response, most of us are quite envious of anyone who possesses the balls to actually give it.

Example two

Oh dear. One could argue that this response is worse than saying 'fuck off', for the following reasons:

- Too much detail makes people feel nervous.
- Fellow talk partner now feels obligated to enquire after Auntie Linda's wellbeing and congratulate Georgia even though they have never met them.
- No one cares about their co-workers' sodding extension plans.

Example three

Good, thanks – went to the pub, hung out with family. It was nice!

In contrast to the first two examples, this person gives a perfect response. It ticks all the right boxes:

- Moderate level of detail.
- Pub and family = relatable activities.
- Concludes the conversation nicely.

After this quick interaction, both participants can now get on with their respective days! Lovely stuff!

Hairdressers

Absolute PRIME territory for small talk – in fact, there is no smaller talk than in a hair salon. It is minute.

If you are not a small-talk fan you need to establish your position on the first visit. If you let your guard down and engage in small talk you will be earmarked as someone who enjoys chit-chat, therefore making it necessary to change salons frequently.

Take a look at the encounter below:

Give nothing away and try to REMAIN SILENT. Remember you are under no obligation to ask the stylist about their holiday. Stay strong and do not crack!

DAMMIT!

Congratulations! Now put down your magazine and get ready to hear the full itinerary of Lydia's two-week jaunt to Cancún.

Neighbours

Neighbours are top contenders for small talk. You probably see them often, don't know them very well, but need to keep them on side.

Fortunately, because seeing neighbours corresponds with exiting or entering your house, you can usually keep the encounter brief under the premise that you need to be somewhere or are coming home after a hard day's work.

Good topics for neighbourly chat include: the increase of dog poo in the area, hearing strange noises in the night, new neighbours moving in/ slagging off problem neighbours (accompanied by tutting), the number of loft conversions currently under construction and, my personal favourite, bin-day discussions.

Now bear in mind that discussing bins can be very helpful, especially when you only have a bi-monthly recycling collection. Neighbourly interactions help me avoid the catastrophic situation of missing recycling day and being left with four weeks' worth of recycling. The number of wine bottles on view by this point is embarrassing and starts to tarnish my wholesome reputation.

Public transport

Imagine this scenario . . .

You are standing on the station platform, waiting for your train. You have arrived in good time and purchased what I like to refer to as a 'train pack', consisting of various snacks, magazines and drinks. You remembered your headphones and your phone battery is fully charged. You may even have bought a nice hot latte! You are looking forward to two hours of peace and quiet – *on your own*.

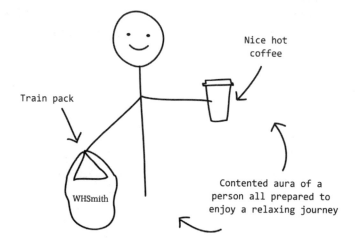

Train pack

Nice hot coffee

WHSmith

Contented aura of a person all prepared to enjoy a relaxing journey

But oh, what's this?

Two minutes before your train is due, you inadvertently lock eyes with a vague acquaintance, let's say an old school mate you've just de-friended on Facebook.

You don't know them very well and have nothing to say to them, but ignoring them completely would be rude. Before you know what you're doing, you've called out to them!

MORON!

The train pulls into the station and you have no choice but to board together. For once you are praying for a busy carriage so you're forced to say your goodbyes and split up. Unfortunately, the carriage is empty. You do a little 'shall we sit here?' dance, knowing that neither of you wants to sit together.

You enquire politely where each other is headed, which of course is the same destination, so you're taking the full two-hour train journey together. Joy.

You can now look forward to spending the entire time locked in an awkward conversation that you give zero fucks about. You cannot look at your magazine because that would appear rude, and you cannot eat your snacks because it feels too intimate to shovel crisps into your gob in front of a near-stranger (and also because you brought Nice 'n' Spicy Nik Naks, which stink and make you look like a child).

Taxis

I don't mind taxi small talk – this is because I usually only get taxis when I am slightly inebriated, and being slightly inebriated increases my desire to chat nonsense with strangers.

However, I am also conscious that night-time taxi drivers must have to witness a lot of terrible behaviour from drunk passengers, so I often ask how they cope dealing with people who are shouting, swearing, puking and generally being rude and obnoxious.

Being a model passenger I express disgust at such stories and act horrified at the absolute mindless behaviour of lesser mortals (despite actually having behaved in exactly the same way myself).

Taxi drivers seem to love me, though, as do I love them.

The supermarket

The supermarket presents a potentially hellish situation in which you may be faced with several small bouts of small talk (as if one isn't enough to deal with).

Bumping into an acquaintance once is OK (in a way). Just greet the person and move on, right?

But things start to feel more awkward when you turn the corner into the next aisle and there they are again! Whilst fumbling around for something to say you look into each other's shopping baskets, searching for a conversation-starter. They are buying organic veggies and you are buying a Pot Noodle and a bottle of Sauvignon Blanc. It's so exposing! It's a shopping basket that says 'I'm pathetic and disgusting'.

The third encounter by the spaghetti hoops in aisle 7 is particularly painful.

You both edge away slowly (laughing nonsensically about nothing). Things have become so awkward that you cannot risk the possibility of another encounter. They already know you are a disgusting Pot Noodle eater and now they also think you are a weirdo with no social skills!

There is nothing else for it. Put your basket down and run, run like the wind! You do not deserve your Pot Noodle and wine evening!

FUN FAMILY CAMPING TRIPS

I love the camping season, don't you? All around us wholesome families are frantically purchasing blow-up mattresses, enamel mugs, torches, antiseptic hand gel and enough wine boxes to kill five medium-sized horses.

They cannot wait to get their tents up! They have visions of fairy lights, bunting, marshmallow-toasting, singing around the campfire and making those chocolate banana things you wrap in foil that turn out horrid.

Now I'm sorry to have to tell you this, but they are COMPLETELY FUCKING DELUDED. Just in case you're thinking of making a similar ~~mistake~~ trip, please note:

1. It will take you approximately five hours to pack your car for a two-night stay and you will have had thirty-seven different arguments before even leaving the house.

2. When you arrive at the campsite you will feel optimistic, capable and ready to face anything – just like Bear Grylls!

Not sure what this animal is meant to be. Was going to be a camel but don't really get them in rural England.

3. You will feel slightly less like Bear Grylls when the Sainsbury's driver arrives delivering essential supplies of Prosecco, halloumi and minted lamb kebabs.

4. You will feel more like what you actually are – a middle-class twat on a camping trip.

5. You will have loads of nice food to eat but the children will exist entirely on a diet of crisps and Capri-Sun.

6. There will be so much to do! Make a list so you don't forget anything . . .

Things I like about camping...

1. Getting drunk in a field
2. Sausages
3. I hate everything else 🙁

7. It will be so lovely to see the kids being at one with nature (pissing against the trees and hitting each other with sticks) that it will seem like a good idea to let them stay up long past bedtime. They should sleep in later the next day so it will be fine!

8. You will drink wine from mugs and dance around the campfire like you're at a 90s rave. Why not put your Care Bear onesie on? You are crazy! You are so much fun! You are unstoppable!

9. YAWN. Even Rave Bear gets tired eventually. Time to say goodnight. Oops . . . did you forget you had to sleep in a tent rather than your comfy, cosy bed? *sad face*

10. You have a lovely blow-up mattress but you will fall/get kicked off it in the middle of the night and sleep pushed up against the lining of the tent on top of a spiky rock.

11. You will wake up at 3 a.m. and really need a wee but be too cold and lazy to find the toilet. You will feel very glad you brought the kids' potty . . .

[FYI I would certainly never do this, I just imagine some people might. I would also never wee into the discarded mug I had been drinking wine out of all evening, as that would be a very disgusting thing that only extremely uncouth people do.]

12. Despite going to bed three hours later than usual, your kids will wake up at 4.30 a.m. because of the BASTARD SUN.

13. You will momentarily want to be dead.

14. But you will power on because CAMPING IS FUN!
You will all enjoy the nature walk if it kills you.

15. You will watch your kids running, playing, getting filthy dirty and enjoying doing everything that kids should do and you will feel all warm and fuzzy and happy.

16. Well done for being such an excellent parent! Please proceed home to enjoy some lovely, lovely technology.

17. Now it's time to enjoy doing something lovely for yourself – like six loads of laundry.

18. Wipe the whole experience from your memory, clear all the horror out, because we all know you'll be doing it again! The kids love it, right, and you love it too, don't ya?! YOU HAD A REALLY GREAT TIME!

PROCRASTINATOR EXTRAORDINAIRE

There are two types of people in this world. Sensible people with a good work ethic, and procrastinators (AKA idiots).

Sensible person

Ooh, a task. The deadline is not for a while, but if I start now I'll have plenty of time to get it all done!

Tasky McTaskface

It usually becomes clear which camp you fall into during your school years. I was a fly-by-the-seat-of-my-pants type of student. I couldn't even get my act together for the most important piece of work I ever had to do – my dissertation. I stayed up writing it through the night, went out to get it bound at first light and handed it in half asleep. The sensible people had it finished two weeks before the deadline and enjoyed a relaxing end to university, partying and seeing friends. I cried a lot.

Now that I'm older and wiser and have a job and responsibilities, I still do the exact same thing.

The scope to procrastinate in the workplace can depend on your line of work. An office job presents many opportunities, which increase when, for example, your boss is out for the day or you're 'working from home'. Everybody knows that 'working from home' means loosely monitoring your emails whilst watching *This Morning*.

Procrastination is a peak problem for people who work for themselves because there is no one to observe or reprimand them. The internet becomes their oyster. I am now self-employed and work from home – the procrastinator's ideal habitat!

I try to kid myself that it's fine to leave everything to the last minute because I work well under pressure – but that's a lie because it's actually a horribly stressful way to get things done. What's really interesting is that even whilst writing a chapter about procrastination, I have procrastinated to an impressively high degree. In fact, maybe even more than normal (for research purposes, obviously). Whilst typing these very words I am simultaneously thinking that I could be ordering a new pair of trainers. Amazing.

Sometimes I'm shocked at how devious my brain can be. I can sit down at my desk fully intending to be productive and then suddenly up pops the Distraction Devil, intent only on luring me away from the task in hand.

I do not know where he gets this stuff from! I have absolutely zero intention of getting a hot tub.

However, just out of curiosity, I can't help but wonder how much they cost and how much maintenance is involved . . . it would be fun at parties, I guess (I never have parties).

Twenty minutes later I'm astounded to find myself downloading a how-to-speak-Korean app on my phone. I've also set my new puppy up with an Instagram account. There is literally no real benefit to setting a dog up with an Instagram account – it is utterly pointless and makes you look like a twat. However, it seemed more pressing than writing this book.

[Note to my editor: sorry about all of this.]

When my husband gets home he enquires as to how my day went.

It's amazing how productive you can be in other areas of your life when you have a larger, more pressing task to complete!

Sadly, my husband doesn't really share my enthusiasm. He thinks that the best way to get a task done is to actually do the task, and not by reorganising your bookcase in colour order so it looks like a rainbow.

Boring!

I quite like the early stage of procrastination, when you can pretty much enjoy wasting time without feeling too stressed because your deadline is AGES away, right?

The problems only start when I hit the midway point between receiving the task and the task needing to be complete.

A little niggle begins to infiltrate my brain. Distraction Devil's nemesis, Sensible Angel, starts whispering to me . . .

Sensible Angel is full of good advice! She knows I should have finished 50% of the task by now, but I find her unsettling.

I am no longer close enough to the start of the task to enjoy doing nothing, yet nor am I close enough to the deadline to actually bother working.

I hate this bit – it's both depressing and non-productive!

Let's take a look at how I fill my day:

A breakdown of my working day

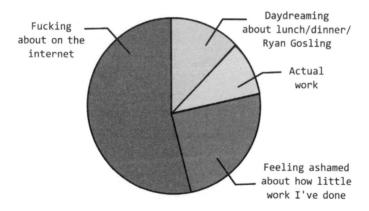

I am still mostly doing nothing, but the really concerning part is that I am spending more time feeling ashamed for not doing anything, rather than *actually* working, and that shame is basically ruining my fun.

I could fix the problem and lower my stress levels by simply increasing the amount of work I'm doing, but guess what?

I. Don't. Want. To.

So here we sit, in stalemate. All of us miserable.

Other people start to clock my apathy and try to be helpful . . .

I start trying a bit harder. Making lists can be really helpful!

Except I'm still not doing the actual bloody task! There only needs to be one item on the list:

1. Get the fuck on with it.

At this point I try and motivate myself with rewards for doing small chunks of work.

For example, Sensible Angel may say, 'Do one hour's worth of solid work without looking at Instagram and you can have a biscuit!'

And I try, I really do try, but Distraction Devil is all like 'Pssst, she is not the boss of you . . .'

Next thing I know, I'm crying in the corner having eaten an entire pack of chocolate Hobnobs.

As the deadline approaches, the nonchalance decreases as I am suddenly hit with what I like to refer to as THE FEAR.

However enjoyable procrastinating can be in the early stages, pay the bills or ace the exams it does not.

THE FEAR can be fed by many possible consequences: failure, losing money, letting people down, getting the sack, etc. Personally I find the prospect of public humiliation pretty motivating.

Sensible Angel begins to get pretty damn real – even Distraction Devil is terrified of her.

There is nothing else for it. I have no choice but to DO SOME HARDCORE WORK. I put my phone away, turn the Wi-Fi off and arm myself with the tools I need for the job!

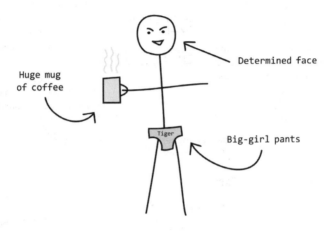

Huge mug of coffee

Determined face

Big-girl pants

Tiger

And I'm not going to lie. It's awful. It's always awful.

Do I regret leaving everything to the last minute? Of course.

Will I leave it until the last minute next time? Of course.

Because this is how the process works for the procrastinator. It is one never-ending circle of pain.

CIRCLE OF PAIN

Get a task → Task feels daunting → Mess about on the internet → Feel ashamed of self → More internet but with shame in background → Impending deadline → Sudden enjoyment of housework → THE FEAR → Do all the work in three days whilst caffeine-fuelled anxious mess → Realise could have done a better job → Won't ever do that again → Get a task

Every. Single. Time.

[End note: hot-tub costs vary but an average tub costs around £5k to buy and around £1 per day to run. You're welcome.]

GET A PUPPY, THEY SAID

'I want a puppy, I want a puppy, I want a puppy!!'

That was my husband's constant plea and the kids were only slightly better.

I was the semi-reticent member of the family because although puppies are cute, I knew that I would be the one doing the vast majority of the hard work. Everyone else was super keen (obviously).

Anyway, a couple of months ago we decided to 'just go and see some puppies' and have a think about it. That was my first mistake. Unless you have a heart made of stone you don't 'just go and see some puppies' without losing your mind over them. Oh my life, they were beautiful!

Anyway, long story short, we signed up for a little cockapoo puppy called Sasha. It didn't take long before other people started doing that annoying thing of telling you how awful it would be, how they would be up all night and destroy your house.

'It's just like having a new baby,' they said.

It can't be that bad! I thought.

I found out that I was wrong. It can be that bad. In fact, sometimes it can be worse.

For example, when you're standing outside in the garden at 5 a.m. in your dressing gown, it's pitch black and pissing down and you are calling 'WEE

WEEEEES . . . WEE WEEEEES' in a silly high-pitched voice whilst your dog looks at you like you're a total moron.

Then after ten minutes of staring at you and running round the garden like a wind-up toy on acid you go inside, and she promptly does a massive wee all over the floor.

Or like the time she got explosive diarrhoea and jumped in it and then ran around the house covering everything with her poo paws (whilst looking very pleased with herself).

In these moments, you start to wonder why the hell you went and fucked it up for yourself – again. Just when you had finally got your kids toilet trained and sleeping through the night!

Another horrific thing I quickly discovered about my puppy is that she likes to eat her own shit. If I spot her doing a poo I literally have to race after her and fight her away from it, such is her ambition to consume it.

I'm also not allowed to wear slippers any more. They're too enticing. Especially my bunny-rabbit ones with the ears – she wants to murder them! Even my dressing gown is a temptation. So are ALL the shoes. She wants to eat everything, actually.

Chairs, books, toys, the floorboards. She has a good go at eating people too.

Then she eats her food so quickly that she pukes it back up and eats that too! She looks dead happy with herself, as if she's just worked out a way to get a BOGOF dinner. I guess it is kind of clever. If you like eating vomit.

My dog's favourite foods...

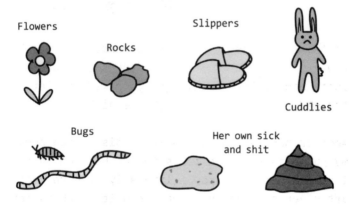

Flowers

Rocks

Slippers

Cuddlies

Bugs

Her own sick and shit

So all in all my puppy is very, very disgusting.

Fortunately, there is a flipside: her face is super cute, she is really bloody adorable *and* she loves me so much!

For example, when I come home and announce my arrival to my kids, their reaction is generally something like this:

When my puppy sees me come home her reaction is best described as ecstatic. In fact, she often pisses herself in excitement. Sometimes she pisses herself in excitement to see me even when I've only been upstairs for three minutes, brushing my teeth.

On one level this is annoying because I now have to clean up her piss. On another level it is amazing as I have never, ever (to my knowledge) had anyone else wet themselves because they love me so much. I am truly touched!

She wants to be with me EVERYWHERE. I have been waiting years to go to the toilet without an audience, but if I try and shut the door she cries and cries until I come out again.

I also feel like I've been transported into a different world I never really knew existed before. Becoming a dog owner is like joining a secret gang.

When I go out for a walk with her, people talk to me ALL the time. Because, wow – how much do people love dogs?! Compared to having a new baby the attention is off the scale. As a new puppy owner I literally get mobbed – it makes every journey take ten times as long! I had about twenty people crowd round me (OK, the dog) the other day and I felt like Taylor Swift.

I feel so proud. No one was ever this nice about my actual children!

And I talk to other people about their dogs too. After years of avoiding eye contact with people in the street, I no longer have that option. I greet many of the dogs we've met at the park by name; I have no idea what their owners are called, but who cares?

As dog owners, you instantly have a common interest and you learn to have the same conversations again and again and again.

What's her name?

How old is he/she?

What type of dog is he/she?

And then you awkwardly talk to your dog, like they understand English, hoping they won't show you up by being unfriendly to the other person's dog.

Then you keep watching and smiling and making idle dog chitter-chatter whilst the dogs sniff each other's privates. Which is all very well unless you have a loud small child with you who likes to shout a detailed account of what they are doing to anyone within a 3-mile radius.

It's the done thing now to teach kids the proper names for genitalia, which is all very well and good, but in instances like this, it just feels kind of wrong.

Anyway, the upshot of this whole puppy ownership malarkey is that I adore it. I really do. It's doing me good. I'm glad to have the excuse to get out and walk her every day.

It's doing the kids good, too – I have never seen them so besotted! They are kind and gentle (OK, maybe not gentle – she is definitely learning to be a very tolerant dog) and head over heels for her, and it makes my heart swell.

So despite the early starts and the mopping up of wee and poo, I'm there, I'm sold. I have time in my life and the space in my heart for this gorgeous girl and we are so glad she's part of our family.

In fact, sometimes I start to wonder if perhaps I love the dog more than anybody else . . .

Then there are days like today, when she's left long trails of runny poo around the garden and we are cooking up plain rice for her tea to try and help her poor little tummy recover. My eldest comes in from outside, 'Mummy, I've just slipped over in all this gross dog poo!' he yells. So I chuck his clothes in the wash and send him off to clean up.

Then there is a call from upstairs. 'Mummy, I did a poo in the shower!'

Perhaps I've misheard – how can that actually happen? I mean, in the shower?! Seriously – WTF?

So I say, 'WHAT?! I think I heard you wrong – what did you say?!'

And he says, in a not-at-all-sorry but more impressed-with-himself type of way . . .

So I set off upstairs to scrape a massive turd out of the shower. FML.

Turns out kids and dogs are pretty alike, and in the grand scheme of things, what difference does one more bum-hole make?

HOW TO HAVE A BEACH BODY

Just enjoy yourself!
No one even cares what you look like.
They are all just looking at
their phones anyway!

10 GODAWFUL THINGS ABOUT GROUP CHATS

In the good old days before the invention of mobile phones, communication options were much more limited. If you wanted to speak to someone outside of school hours they had to call your landline and be directed to you via the operator (your mum). If you wanted a private conversation, you would have to take the handset into the hall and try and shut the door as much as you could over the phone wire. Everything seemed simpler – if you made a plan to meet up with someone in town, you simply had to be there in the right place at the right time or everything would go wrong. There were no last-minute messages of 'I can't make it' or 'Actually, let's meet here instead'.

Plans were solid. Clubs let you in at fifteen. Life was good.

Of course it wasn't all good. There was the arrival of the dreaded itemised BT bill where, when the total was particularly bad, my dad would hit the roof and make me and my sisters go through it line by line, highlighting which calls were ours so we could pay for them out of our pocket money. You had to be honest because he threatened to phone up any unaccounted-for phone numbers and ask them who they were (which was actually a very effective threat).

The invention of mobile phones and text messages changed all that. I got my first phone in 1999 – the Nokia 5110. Everyone had the same model and we all customised them with tasteless combinations of keypads and fascias that you could buy from the market for £5. My favourite combo was a transparent turquoise case and rainbow jelly numbers. It was disgusting and I loved it. Finally, I could phone anyone I liked at any time of the day – it opened up a whole new world of opportunity.

Nowadays, however, no one really phones anyone any more. We have grown accustomed to being almost fearful of a ringing phone.

It's either PPI, the water board, or worst of all someone calling for 'a chat' – why can't they just text like a normal person?!

I NEVER answer the phone to a number I don't recognise. Instead I wait until it's finished ringing and then google the number to try and work out who it is and what they might want.

Yet also gone are the days of the excitement of receiving a text message. My biggest bugbear with modern communication is that there are now just too many methods by which to do it. I'll have a recollection of a friend messaging me about something but I can't figure out where the message was. Was it via text, Messenger, Twitter?! Did they email me, tag me in the comments of a humorous Facebook post or was it an Instagram DM?! I don't know where I am any more!

You may think this makes me sound popular, but it's not that – the vast majority of these comments and messages aren't very interesting. In fact, most of them come via the worst communication method of all: the dreaded group chat.

Whether you like them or not, the chances are you are a member of several.

Book groups, sports clubs, local friends, university friends, family, work, communities, random surprise parties, Beavers, babysitting circles and school parents. The list goes on. And on. And on.

Group chats can be excellent when they're used in a functional way. They have saved my bacon on many occasions. Largely by stopping me sending my children into school in their uniforms on 'dress like a pirate day', or any one of the fifty-seven fancy-dress days the school has over the course of the year.

They are also useful for staying in touch with small groups of good friends. But that is where it ends.

I am a member of approximately two groups that I actively enjoy. The rest I, errr . . . don't. No offence. Here's why:

Most of it is boring as fuck

People can put you into any group they like without your permission, and 90% of the time it will be something shit like 'Daniel's leaving present!' or 'Betsy's 6th birthday party!' (which incidentally turns out to be at a hideous soft play centre at 6.30 p.m. on a Friday evening. Sigh).

Sometimes I physically shudder when I see a notification pop up on my phone to say I've been added to a new group.

HELP ME!

People are always being so stupid!

Someone in the group says something like 'Reminder: there is a rugby game this Sunday – let me know if you can't make it!'

The key word here is 'CAN'T'.

Next thing you know there's a stream of comments from people saying 'I can!', 'Yes, I can!', 'I can too!'

Errr, they said 'let me know if you <u>CAN'T</u> make it!' (which FYI is the opposite of 'can'). Learn to fucking read.

There are too many side-conversations

This is perhaps the worst. Why do some people use a large group chat to have a conversation about something no one else has any interest in?

No, Penny, we don't care what time you're picking Jess up from Sophie's house, or whether she needs a booster seat or if she'll have had lunch yet or what her shoe size is.

Here's an idea – how about starting a private chat and stop wasting everyone else's time?

They are full of people you don't know

How on god's earth do you interact with a random telephone number? What sort of jokes do they like? What are their boundaries? Who are they? They could be murderers FFS! Are you even safe in your own home any more??

And lurkers

You know that person who reads everything but never comments. It feels creepy and weird and like they're probably laughing at you behind your back.

After a while you might forget they're there and then, perish the thought, send a message like 'Martin was being a total twat last night' to a group that Martin is actually in. Awkward.

When you try and be funny no one replies!

When you do actually have time on your hands and feel like joining in with a bit of group 'banter', you make what you think is a really funny joke and guess what?

Tumbleweed.

Not one bastard replies!

Everyone was laughing at Emma's not even vaguely funny joke yesterday – how come they're ignoring you?

Read receipts are evil

Plus you can't even pretend they just haven't read your joke yet because you can SEE that it's been read . . . and ignored. Oh the shame!

Sponsorship requests

This is going to make me sound mean because giving money to charity is really great. Doing impressive stuff to raise money for charity is also really great. Setting up direct debits to support your favourite charities is spot on. But I'm so sick of people I don't know asking me to sponsor them to do something nice and unimpressive like go on a short walk. Why not just quietly give some of your own money to charity and piss off.

You simply can't keep up!

Wake up. Look at phone. 127 new notifications.

WHY?!?

It's certainly not because I'm a social butterfly. Half the time I don't even know what the fuck they're talking about. Something about needing to bake a cake, TV programmes I don't watch, timings of a party my kids aren't invited to, hilarious commentary about a night out I didn't go on.

NO! NO MORE! THIS HAS TO STOP!

The problem is . . .

You can NEVER LEAVE!!!

I know what you're saying now: Oh man, she's being so unreasonable. If she doesn't like the groups she's in then why doesn't she just leave??

I'll tell you why: because you can't 'just leave'.

I mean, what do you say?

'Hello, I'm not really interested in this group any more. I don't like anyone in it and your chat is getting pretty tedious. Thanks for your time, goodbye!'

It'd probably be preferable to just throw your phone in the fire! If you have the balls you could be like my friend Abi, who posted this status on Facebook:

Abi ▓▓▓▓▓▓▓▓▓▓
Wednesday at 18:09 · 👥   •••

Can I ask people not to ever include me in large group messages on messenger about any subject.

She had been added into a large group whereby the perpetrator (yes, that *is* what they are) added all of their random, unrelated friends to one group in order to wish them happy New Year. She had to read through streams of comments from people she had never met wishing her a great 2019. It was the straw that broke the camel's back!

The closest I ever get to throwing in the towel is when I feel slightly emboldened after a particularly annoying spate of messages (and perhaps a gin or two). I think 'Right, that's it, I've had enough!' and I get my phone and I mute the fuck out of everyone!

And it's so nice . . . for a bit. Sort of. I mean, it's kind of nice. You don't have any friends left, you don't get invited to parties and you keep turning up on the wrong date or at the wrong time for everything – BUT at least you are FREE.

But I always go back. I have to. I mean, how else would I know that I need to bring green leggings into school on Tuesday for the class assembly?

It's a survival thing.

BULLSHITTING YOUR WAY THROUGH MEETINGS

One of the worst things about work is meetings. There are too many of them and they go on for too long. There are team catch-ups, company meetings, client meetings, pitches, breakfast meetings, lunch meetings, coffee-shop meetings, performance meetings, meetings about meetings – and they are all equally pointless.

Some of the reasons why meetings are bad:

1. They are boring.
2. They are time-consuming.
3. They lead to more work.
4. They have the potential to publicly expose you as a fraud.
5. Everyone is just bum-licking.

One of the best things to happen at work is when a meeting gets cancelled! One of the worst things that can happen at work is when you bump into a colleague in the corridor and they say something like this . . .

Buckle up and put on your best 'I look interested' face because you are in for the long haul. There will probably be about 200 slides to get through and only ten of them will be vaguely interesting!

Meetings that you go to voluntarily can be dispiriting. However, it is very difficult to get out of a meeting when it's sprung on you. Generally you should decide on whether you need to be at a meeting by asking yourself the following questions:

1. Does this meeting even need to happen?
2. What can I add by being there?
3. Will there be snacks?

In my experience it's rare that the meeting needs to happen and even if it does, do you really think you'll have anything intelligent to contribute? Probably not. The third decider is an interesting one – if the meeting is internal, the snacks won't be happening; you may get a tepid jug of tap water if you're lucky, and at best someone may offer to make a round of tea. If a client is coming, you can cross your fingers for an M&S sandwich platter or at least a tray of fancy(ish) biscuits.

You may think that having good snacks at a meeting makes it more appealing; however, they can be a poisoned chalice because they actually just make it incredibly difficult to concentrate, and it is almost impossible to maintain an aura of professionalism whilst eating a Viennese whirl.

BLAH BLAH sales
BLAH BLAH budget
BLAH BLAH targets

Everyone else
concentrating

You thinking about
Jammie Dodgers

You need to watch out because at some point in the meeting someone may randomly turn to you and say something along the lines of 'So, Katie, what do you think?'

You will start to panic and look down at your notes, hoping that they will provide some clues as to what the meeting has been about. Unhelpfully, your notebook will be blank and covered in crumbs.

There is nothing else for it. You will have to throw one of your colleagues under a bus!

Sorry, Dave, but it's a dog-eat-dog world out there and people shouldn't be putting Jammie Dodgers out in meetings if they want to be taken seriously!

I once went to a meeting where they had put out retro chocolate biscuits as some sort of homage to the 1980s. Think Clubs, Penguins, Tunnock's Tea Cakes and, get this – WAGON WHEELS!! I hadn't had a Wagon Wheel for decades, so you can imagine how much information I was absorbing in that meeting – fucking none.

As the meeting comes to an end you may start to relax, relieved that you can go back to your desk and look at ASOS for the rest of the afternoon . . . However, please keep your eyes down! It is a very bad situation if you find the meeting organiser looks at you and says something like 'Could you write up and email round the minutes, please?' when all you've written is a list of your top five favourite biscuits.

I mean, personally I'd be more interested in an email chain discussing biscuit preferences, but each to their own.

Moving on – the absolute worst meeting to find yourself in isn't a boring one you have no interest in, it's one you have to actively participate in. It's these . . .

The very thought of them makes me shudder in horror.

No one likes them.

NO ONE!

Except the organiser (who, coincidentally, always seems to be wearing glasses which are way too big for their face). They only like them because they

have no ideas of their own and believe - wrongly
- that organising brainstorms makes them seem
creative and kooky.

The main reason to dislike brainstorming sessions
is because of the pressure to come up with great
ideas - on the spot. You can't just sit there
silently, you have to say something! You don't
want it to be too sensible and obvious or you'll
seem dull, and you don't want it to be too
nonsensical or you'll seem weird.

Also, the meeting organiser is incorrect. There
are wrong answers and there are also stupid ideas.
In fact, nearly everything uttered in a brainstorm
is completely useless.

Another terrible thing about meetings is you may be required to actually chair one.

Most of the meetings I went to in my professional life were client meetings where I would be required to present the results of the very expensive advertising campaigns we had been running for them. The problem I found when compiling such presentations was that the results were often quite shit, and it looked like we had wasted a large amount of the client's money.

In these meetings the aim was to prove to a client that you were adding value to their business and not just pissing their money up the wall. The gist was always something along the lines of:

'We have paid you 3 million quid – what have you done with it?'

Sigh. Everyone is always so obsessed with return on investment, but where's the fun in that?!

The tactic to employ in such situations is PowerPoint. Some will say, 'You shouldn't need to use slides if you know what you're talking about' and they would be right. PowerPoint is basically the visual distraction a presenter uses to help disguise the fact that they have no idea what they're talking about.

First up, you're going to need a slide headed 'Objectives'. Everyone will be impressed you have a meeting with objectives. It doesn't matter what your objectives are, just make sure you don't tell them the real one:

The real objective is certainly not to be completely truthful with the client. You do not want them to know that the cost per sale of a toaster was a very unimpressive £47,987.

In this situation you need to do something called 'putting a positive spin on it' – also known as 'polishing a turd'. This is where you bamboozle everyone with impressive slides that make it look like you are very clever and hard-working.

The best way to do this is with graphs. Everyone is impressed by pretty graphs that go upwards. Just make sure you plot the good figures, not the ones everyone actually wants you to include.

If you spot someone writing down something you're saying, you get a bonus point for making some semblance of sense – well done, superstar!

There will always be one arsehole jobsworth client, though – let's call her Sarah – who is set on bringing you down by asking thinly veiled passive-aggressive questions . . .

You have several get-out clauses:

1. Blame everything on an error in the tracking technology.
2. Start banging on about how generating awareness will lead to sales at a later date.
3. Throw Dave under the bus – again.
4. Suggest an ice-breaker game to lighten the mood.

My personal favourite is number four. Everyone
hates ice-breaker games, so they'll want the
meeting to end as soon as humanly possible.

Everyone except Dave.

YOU WILL ALWAYS FIND SOMEONE DOING
SOMETHING BIGGER AND BETTER THAN YOU

IT DOESN'T MEAN THAT YOUR
ACHIEVEMENTS ARE NOT IMPORTANT

SOCIAL MEDIA TWATTERY

Social media for me is a bit like tequila. Feels like it should be fun, but leaves you with an icky taste in your mouth.

Sure, it has many positives, the chief one being that it allows us to swap and share funny animal videos and easily keep in touch with loved ones. Also I, like many others, have built a career out of social media, so I can hardly slag it off too much, can I?

I can if I like.

You see, I often wonder how perfectly lovely people can become so loathsome online.

Twat ... boring ... idiot ... no one cares ... fuck off!

Me scrolling through social media

239

What is it about Facebook that seems to bring out the inner wanker in people?

Now, to be entirely upfront, I very much include myself in this group too. I am well aware that I have sometimes (often) behaved like a total twat online. It is almost impossible not to, because the top two uses of Facebook are showing off and attention-seeking – neither of which are particularly attractive character traits.

Let's look at a few examples below:

 Lucy Hopkins
SOME PEOPLE HAVE A RIGHT FUCKING NERVE!!

 7 people like this

 Georgia Young
U ok hun??

 Lucy Hopkins
I'll inbox u babes. Can't say on here x

If you want to be an attention-seeker then fine, but it's not OK to go all cryptic on us! If the wheels of your life are truly falling off then let the rest of us know the juicy details, please!

Here's another classic:

Gavin Thomas is 😞 feeling sad
at Brighton Hospital, A&E department

👍 🤍 😞 3 people like this

See how Gavin provides zero information? He's
goading us in the hope of eliciting a stream
of 'Oh my god, Gavin, what's wrong?!!?' type
comments. Gavin has most likely just burnt
his tongue on a hot cup of tea because if you
were actually dying then would checking in to
hospital on Facebook be top of your priority list?
Actually, for Gavin, it would probably be the
silver lining.

Next up we have the incessant posters. They
cannot go anywhere or do anything without
posting an update for everyone else to see. I'm
pointing the finger at myself circa 2008/9 here,
which was obviously a very riveting period of my
life. I wish I could go back in time and give
myself a good slap because literally no one must
have cared about what snacks I was eating and
the specific time I was planning to consume a
banana.

Katie
April 9, 2008

just thoroughly enjoyed some laughing cow cheese dippers

Like   Comment

Write a comment...

Katie
August 7, 2009

Buzzing off vimto and astro belts

Like   Comment   Share

Write a comment...

Katie
March 11, 2008

is saving her banana until 3pm

Like   Comment

Write a comment...

WTAF?!

Also rather high up on the scale of irritating social media users are new parents. Aside from the birth announcement and the odd milestone pic, there are very few updates about your amaaaazing kid that anyone actually wants to know about. We really, really do not need to see 1,671 photos of them consuming a piece of broccoli. As for poo pictures – NO. That is all kinds of wrong.

Maybe their delusion that they're the first people in the world to ever procreate is due to sleep deprivation. Those who have zero excuses, however, are the happy couple.

The happy couple is basically the same as the new parents – except worse. Their public declarations of love can make people be a little bit sick into their own mouths.

242

Take a look at this:

My absolute world! Thank you for my new Chanel handbag **Ben Lawrence**. Words can't express what you mean to me! 💜
#blessed #lovedup #luckygirl #pinchme

👍 Like 💬 Comment ➤ Share

👍 💜 😊 13 people like this

There are so many things wrong with this post that I don't know where to start. It is enough to make you want to delete your entire account and go and live a simple life on a remote farm in Tanzania.

A wise man once said, 'There is no better sign of a happy relationship than its complete lack of reference on social media', and he was not wrong.

Now we get to the number one use of Facebook/ Instagram, which is letting people know how amazingly successful you are and how well your life is going:

So tired after a nine-hour flight with zero sleep but I still have a full heart! #makingmemories #barbados #holibobs #wanderlust

👍 Like 💬 Comment ➤ Share

👍 💜 😄 37 people like this

A beautiful demonstration of the humblebrag!

You see a happy shot of a wonderful family holiday, right?

The subtext here is: see how happy we are, see how well we're looking, and mostly . . . na na na naaaaaaaaa na, I can afford a nicer holiday than you!

But what you do not see is that the kids were promised three ice-creams each for their lacklustre smiles. You do not know that ten minutes earlier they'd had a full-on fist fight over a plastic fork. You cannot see the sunburn or the eye-bags because the photo has been filtered to fuck. You have no idea that Mummy and Daddy have been constantly bickering since they arrived in Barbados and are now on the brink of divorce.

You do not know anything at all because the photo says nothing except 'Look at us, aren't we fucking happy!'

Similarly we all post about amazing exam results, parents' evenings, awards, promotions and sodding running routes with new personal bests – but where is the flipside? It's no wonder, when things don't go to plan, that we start feeling like we're the only ones who are struggling.

Now the vast majority of us share such photos, and it's nice to be proud of yourself and your family, and hopefully you have a network of people on social media who are good friends who will be pleased to see you enjoying life.

But sometimes I think we have to question our motivation behind what and how much we post. If we don't get the balance right, our lives can start to seem like one big long string of social media content.

Now that's not to say it's easy. I mean, is it even possible to go out for cocktails and not post about it?!

Checking the likes and comments, seeking comfort in the validation you can feel from a popular post, finding disappointment and regret when you post something that gets few responses . . . this can all start to affect your wellbeing and make you feel rather anxious.

There is a simple answer here: cut back or switch off. But that can feel like an impossible task. Sometimes I get my phone out of my bag to check the time and find that I have lost twenty minutes in an internet black hole. I put my phone back in my bag and I still have no idea what the time is.

Then there is the issue of getting to sleep at a decent hour . . .

In all honesty, I think we'd probably be a lot happier without social media. Frequently I look at other people's snaps and status updates and wonder how they are holding it together so well. And that is even when I KNOW most of it is bollocks.

It's hard enough to make sense of as an adult. How on god's earth are teenagers supposed to cope with it?

In the olden times before social media and smartphones, being a teenager was hard, but everything was left at the school gates. Now there is a twenty-four-hour slide show of the parties you're not invited to, your ex with his new girlfriend, everyone else's pictures getting more likes than yours, the mean comments, the put-downs and the exclusion. I have no idea how young people are meant to navigate themselves through such a shit show of twenty-four-hour one-upmanship. I'm fairly sure it would have left me in tatters.

I mean, do you ever spend an hour surfing social media, close it down and then think 'Ahhhh, that was a productive and satisfying use of my precious free time!'

I'll wager not!

I'll wager that you are more likely to feel guilty and jittery.

I'll wager that the vast majority of us have at some point lost many hours trying to win a Facebook argument with someone we don't know over something so inconsequential that we've forgotten what the point we were trying to make even was.

Many times I have caught myself in the midst of getting annoyed about something unimportant and stopped myself and thought – why am I doing this? What good will it actually do?

The internet is so full of annoying and irritating things that sometimes you just need to stop and let them slide on by.

The best way to improve your social media experience is to de-friend and unfollow people and pages or accounts that you don't like, to make the whole experience much more purposeful and enjoyable.

However, the problem with doing this can be twofold: firstly, some of them may be family and friends, and secondly (and more importantly), some of us secretly enjoy hating other people on social media! Ahem.

But scaling back and streamlining can be a very positive thing, because it is all too easy to get lost in a loop of consuming content that brings nothing good or meaningful to your life.

This is an exact conversation I had with my eldest son as he clocked me on my phone a while ago:

Me: *scrolling through Instagram*

8-year-old: Who's that person?

Me: I don't know.

8-year-old: Who's that person?

Me: I don't know.

8-year-old: What's that dog called?

Me: I don't know.

8-year-old: Why are you looking at photos of people and dogs you don't know?

Me: I don't know.

At that very moment I was well and truly put in my place by my own child, who managed to highlight just how bonkers what I was doing was.

We are all still learning, and finding that elusive phone/life/social media balance is bloody hard. However, here are a few things I'm starting to realise:

- A bit of light escapism is good but vacuous scrolling just makes you feel fucking empty.
- Putting your phone out of reach (preferably in another room, possibly in a locked box) allows you to fully relax and switch off.
- It doesn't matter what other people are doing; doing your own thing is more important.
- Social media lies. No one is talking about their failures.
- You do not need anyone else's validation.
- Finally, and perhaps most importantly, friends who look at group photos and share the one where they look amazing and everyone else looks like shit are not actually 'friends' at all.

Awesome night out with my beautiful girl gang! #BFFs #Friends4Eva

👍 Like   💬 Comment   ➡ Share

👍 🤍 😣 2 people like this

FFS take this down! Carly looks like an extra from Dawn of the Dead and I look like a sodding thumb!

THERE'S ALWAYS ONE ...

IT'S OFTEN YOU

MUMS ON THE RAZZ

*** Please note that ALL characters and events in this story are completely fictional and any similarities to real life are COMPLETELY coincidental ***

The older you get, the less inclined you are to want to go out. It's OK, I get it. There is terrifying stuff out there! People are younger and trendier than you, they know how to be fun and are good at 'banter' or whatever that means. (Is it just talking? Did we need a new word for talking?)

By contrast, you prefer sitting at home on your sofa and shouting obscenities at people you don't like on the TV. But that's not much of a life, is it?

But every once in a while you must leave your little hermit cave or else everyone will think you're very boring and you will end up having zero friends.

All hail THE MUMS' NIGHT OUT!

You know the one, right? The one it's taken two and a half years to organise because spontaneity is dead for people over thirty.

Well, tonight's the night and EVERYONE can attend!
You have spent all day staring at your phone,
willing someone to cancel, and so have all of your
friends. No one actually wants to go, but it's too
late now – it's time to get ready!

The problem is that you have absolutely no idea
what the youth of today wear any more. Don't
worry, it's OK to be scared sometimes, it's hard
getting old! Have a shower and then sit on your
bed and spend two hours staring into space. You'll
feel so much better.

Now, you have three options:

1. Wear one of your too small/short/tarty pre-kids clubbing outfits.
2. Wear a flowery tea dress and hope for the best.
3. Stay in and watch telly.

Option 3 is very, very tempting but you could make option 2 work if you wear the right make-up. Put on a bright statement lipstick to detract from your eye-bags and then cover your entire face in Touche Éclat.

TOP TIP! Drink wine whilst you do your make-up because it makes you think you look better.

Time to meet up with your friends. You feel simultaneously reassured and horrified to discover that everyone has gone for outfit option 2 and you are all dressed like a slutty version of Kirstie Allsopp. Apart from Lisa, who went with option 1 and looks a bit like Shirley from *EastEnders*.

Never mind – you've made it out and you feel AMAZING. Look at you all having fun! Someone has even brought a selfie stick (so cool). Make sure you take lots of photos to post on Facebook as evidence of what INCREDIBLY CRAZY PEOPLE you are!

Now, the thing to remember is that as you don't get out much any more, your alcohol tolerance is probably lower than it used to be. You should be careful to drink slowly and NEVER mix your drinks.

Like this, for example . . .

7.31 p.m. pints

8.03 p.m. wine –
red or white or Prosecco
(or all three!)

8.37 p.m.
cocktails

8.59 p.m. trendy craft
beers to look down
with the kids

9.15 p.m. uh-oh,
here comes the Jäger train!

Oooooooops.

Never mind, you'll be OK as long as you remember to have a glass of water between each round . . .

Ooooooops.

So the upshot is that everyone is now rat-arsed.
Someone suggests moving on to a club, which is
obviously the best idea ever.

When you get to the club you should all
proceed directly to the toilet and spend a
considerable amount of time stroking each
other. #FRIENDS4EVA

It can feel tempting to spend the whole night in the loo but you must make the most of your WILD night out. There are SO many fun things to do . . .

Perform some lunges, do shots of tequila, steal someone's jaunty trilby hat, flirt with a hipster.

Why not be a total ROCK STAR and do all of the above simultaneously?

Shit.

You look at your watch – it's only 9.47 p.m.

You are not really a rock star after all. What you are is a (nearly) middle-aged mum making a spectacle of yourself in a slightly naff chain pub.

Where the hell is everybody else?

You find Rachel blagging fags in the smoking area, utterly convinced she has made BFFs with a group of teenage boys.

You find Steph gyrating on a table-top. Lisa is showing photos of her children to the bar staff and – OH GOD – now Rachel has started to hump a pot plant . . .

It's time to leave!

Go and find a late-night McDonald's (actually just a normal one will do as it's still only 10.34 p.m.).

Maccy D's is a great place to stuff your face with chicken nuggets, and also a great place to have an emotional breakdown about a boy who dumped you in 1997.

OK, TAXI!

Steph looks a bit peaky. Put Steph in the back and mouthy Lisa in the front.

Lisa can distract the taxi driver with tedious
chat about school catchment areas whilst Steph
performs a tactical chunder into her handbag like
the classy bird she is.

G'wan, Steph, attagirl!

OK, you're home. You (not me – this is fictional,
remember) might have forgotten your keys or
lost your keys or thrown them at a seagull for
squawking too loudly. You might be hammering down
the door and shouting incoherently through the
letterbox. You might collapse into the hallway
when your pissed-off husband finally gets out of bed
to let you in . . .

You might then feel hungry and stuff your face with an entire six-pack of crisps, because Peter Pan LOVES Quavers . . .

. . . before crawling into bed half clothed for a lovely, lovely long sleep.

BUGGER. Did you forget you had children?

DAILY GRIEVANCES

When I was younger I used to be super chilled. I was messy, easy-going and I'd pretty much get on with anybody. Nowadays I find all those things much more difficult because I am slowly turning into a miserable old bastard.

I think I would be fine for the most part if it wasn't for other people and all the irritating, frustrating things they do.

For example, when I'm out walking it's usually because I have a place to get to, and to get there I have to walk along the street. Other people seem to think that it's OK to stand in the street dawdling, 'having a chat' and blocking the way with their stupid shopping bags.

This is the type of scene I encounter all the time:

When I'm already close to the edge it can take every ounce of strength I have not to react in the following manner:

I didn't always find other people so difficult. When I started university I wasn't at all fazed by the prospect of moving into a flat with a bunch of random people. In fact, I felt confident that I'd probably get on with most of them.

If now, at thirty-nine, I was tasked with cohabiting with six total strangers, I'm pretty sure it would turn into some sort of scaled-down version of the Hunger Games – each of us dying a horrible death by means of various kitchen utensils.

You see, as we age, we become less and less tolerant of other people and the things they do. Take a look at the graph below:

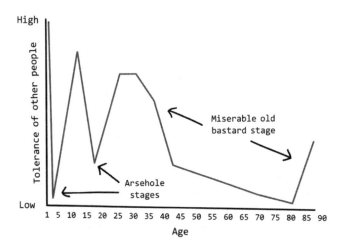

As a baby, you are the most tolerant you'll ever be. You love people – they provide milk and cuddles and smiles – everything you need! Things change significantly in toddlerhood when you are given exciting toys and then expected to 'share nicely now'. WTF?!

Your general demeanour improves from school age and you hit peak niceness aged nine to ten before becoming horrifically angry at life in your teenage years. Things stabilise in your twenties, but when you get to your mid-thirties your tolerance enters a stage of dramatic decline as you start to become 'set in your ways'. You may find that your tolerance of others improves as you approach the end of life; this is because you don't want to die alone, you are going senile or because you have found Jesus Christ and you want to improve your chances of getting into heaven.

As I've got older, I have found that I'm starting to become annoyed with other people in completely illogical ways. For example, I have a favourite café I particularly like to work in, and in that café I have a favourite seat I like to sit in. The other day I arrived there and encountered the following scene:

My favourite seat

Someone else sitting in it

I felt very irritated by that person. Now you may be reading this thinking, it's unreasonable to get annoyed with another person for sitting in a seat in a café you don't own, but I couldn't help it. It was just how I felt.

Part of me wanted to go up to them and inform them that they were sitting in my seat:

MY CHAIR!!!

Yet sadly the constraints of what constitutes normal behaviour meant what I actually had to do was this:

Find another very similar seat

Keep bad thoughts inside head

I drank my flat white in a miserable funk. I didn't bother to get my laptop out as I didn't feel much like working.

For the most part I am able to quash the desire to act on my irrational thoughts, and as such I do still have some friends left.

However, I really enjoy a good old whinge. So here are a few other things that drive me insane:

- People having a loud, boring thirty-minute chat on the phone about nothing whilst they are on the train.

- People who put bags on seats and then act all annoyed when you want to use the seat to sit on.
- People who don't say thank you when you hold the door for them.
- People eating McDonald's when I don't have a McDonald's.
- People who use shared arm-rests and put their elbows right over the edges into MY seat zone.
- People who block roads with their cars whilst they are running 'important' errands.
- People who think they own the parking space outside their house.
- People who park on double yellow lines and then get angry when they get a ticket.
- People who park on the zig-zags outside schools with absolutely no regard for the safety of the children trying to cross the road.
- People who can't be bothered to RSVP.
- People who interrupt you.
- People who talk too much about themselves.
- People who tell really boring stories about people you don't even know.
- People who don't pick up their dog's poo.
- Z-list celebrity yo-yo dieters.
- Weather forecasters getting the weather wrong.
- People who play music/watch vidoes on their phones in public places without even using headphones. WTF?!?!?!?!
- Late people.

- Early people.
- Virtual strangers calling you 'hun'.
- ALSO it's hon not hun!
- Finally, people who ask 'Where's that then?' when you give them the name of a specific place to meet. FUCKING GOOGLE IT, MORON!

I mean, I could go on. I actually posted on Instagram that I could fill an entire book on the subject. Or probably several books . . .

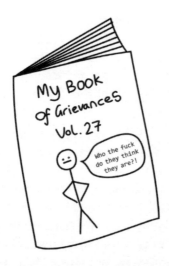

I wasn't sure what people would think but the response was phenomenal. People started sharing all the things that they hated about other people, as well as about life in general. Who knew that sharing things you hate could be so positive. It was inspirational!

My favourite post came from a lady named Shannon. Her grandmother, Nanny Win, had written a list of people she hated off the TV. She has kindly given me permission to include it in this book.

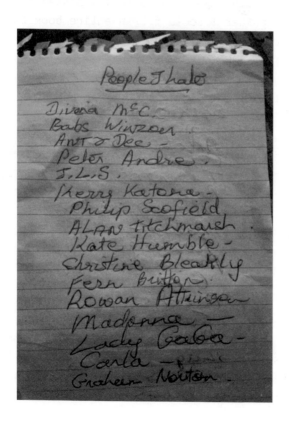

I shared this list and people loved it! They couldn't get enough of Nanny Win and her list of hate!

I was only upset that Nanny Win hadn't written a more detailed account of the reasons why she hated each of these people so much. I mean, what had JLS done to offend her?!

I also got a lot of messages asking 'Who's Carla?!' I asked Shannon to clarify and she revealed it was Carla Connor from *Corrie*. Of course!

It didn't stop there. People were rabid – they started messaging me their own #dailygrievances. Who knew there was so much pent-up anger out there? But the message was clear – it's better to let it out!

[Side note: I have to apologise for the naughty language used in many of these messages – people were obviously very passionate!]

anon. My husband eats soup straight from the saucepan after heating it up. It drives me fucking crazy and I have to put up with the metal spoon scraping the metal of the pan. It's making me close to losing my shit just thinking about it.

@geyvid I'm at a Xmas lunch. Apparently the cheese doesn't come with crackers? Seriously? WTAF?

@stephaniericciardi 7.5 weeks and I'm still fucking waiting for broadband! Pull your finger out BT!!! I can't keep paying for extra data!!!!

@carla_alkhoory People who OVERLY hide their PIN when they're paying for something, even when the machine has little side bits to cover it. CHILL THE FUCK OUT, BRENDA!

@rhiannonmelyn When people don't pull over quick enough to let ambulances pass. JUST GET OUT OF THE WAY!

anon. If you've ever worked in retail/hospitality and it's Christmas and a customer says 'It's a shame you're here on Christmas!' Yes because I'm serving you, Barbara, you absolute cunt!

@i_am_mrs_nelson_ivf Customers making you count the money out of their sweaty hands. Pocket fluff and pubes included.

@heatherandrosieandolive People who know the sex of their baby but won't tell anyone else.

Nobody gives a shit, Sandra, you are not a celebrity!

anon. Absolute bastards that swim 2 or 3 abreast CHATTING!! Fucking talking in the pool. Get yer face in the water, Gladys, and shut the fuck up.

@manversusbaby The awkward unrealistic couple on *Location, Location, Location*. 'Yes, we know you want a four-bedroomed property in central London with a garden and a ballroom but you've got 40 fucking grand, you dopey twats.' And while I'm on it. AUTOCORRECT. Whoever is in charge of autocorrect for the iPhone is a ducking count.

@phe_glover_x The fucking delivery man with the loudest knock, asking me to take parcels for neighbours . . . I feel forced to be neighbourly! YOU HAVE WOKEN MY SLEEPING BABY THAT TOOK ME 2 HOURS OF ROCKING AND SHUSHING TO PUT DOWN!!!!

@dometic_tech People who don't get their wallet out ready at the checkout. FFS. It's hardly a surprise! Duh! You have to actually pay! They put their handbag down. Open the bag. Find the vouchers. Find the wallet. Decide cash or card . . . 'Have you got your loyalty card?' 'Ooh yes, hold on a minute, let me find it'. I don't have a minute! I picked the express till because I will never get this time back!!!

@briannaaohara My toddler has discovered the dog's butthole.

@pipdani87 Space invaders. Fucking nothing worse than being stood in a line waiting and Mavis behind you is so bleedin' close she is literally inhaling strands of my hair with every breath and when I go to pay, how about you come too so you can continue to inhale my skin cells. TAKE TWO FUCKING STEPS BACK, MAVIS!

@jesss_runs Can I just mention my rage at people WITHOUT CHILDREN parking in PARENT SPOTS!!! Argh! WHERE ARE YOUR KIDS, DOUCHEBAG?? IN YOUR POCKET??? Oh, that's right, you don't have any, you're just a total ASSWIPE!

@lisadickson1 Queue jumpers, fucking queue jumpers, they boil my piss!! No it's ok, Susan, you just push in front of me, I've only been here for 20 minutes, you twat. And breathe . . . thanks for that I feel cleansed. In fact, no I'm not cleansed, you have unleashed my inner cunt, drivers who don't use indicators!!! It's like playing a game of give me a fucking clue. Which way you going, dickhead?!?! Now I'm sat watching *I'm a Celebrity Get Me out of Here* getting madder and madder! Nick Knowles wants biting on his cock by a tarantula. Prick.

I love these people! Especially Lisa – she is my spirit animal.

Now, sadly Nanny Win is no longer with us; she passed away in 2011. Shannon assures me she was a real character who trekked through the jungle during World War II from Burma to India before she came to the UK. Apparently she was hilarious and would have loved to have seen this much joy inspired by her excellent list. Here is a picture of the legend herself:

God bless you, Nanny Win!

So what we've learned in this chapter is that anger towards other people, be it irrational or not, is normal (kind of), and letting it all out can be hugely therapeutic and good for the soul!

[Task: Why not try making your own list of hate on the following page. See how much better you feel!]

My Daily Grievances

1.
2.
3.
4.
5.
6.
7.
8.
9.
10.
11.
12.
13.
14.
15.
16.
17.
18.
19.
20.

DON'T RUN FROM YOUR PROBLEMS ...

THEY ARE NEVER AS BAD AS YOU THINK ...

SLEEP, WHERE ART THOU?

It's lovely going to bed. I love bed and I love sleep. The problem is that sleep doesn't always love me. Sometimes I can be so exhausted and almost falling asleep on the sofa and then I'll be like 'Right, I'm super tired, it's time for bed!'

So I'll go upstairs, get my jimjams on and get into bed, looking forward to a lovely long, relaxing sleep and then BAM – I find out my brain has a different plan.

So I'll indulge my brain for a little bit – I
mean, it's nice to have a little catch-up once in
a while, right? Talk about all the ridiculous shit
you've done together, etc. But the problem is my
brain often likes to keep the conversation going
on a lot longer than I do.

After an hour or so I start feeling a little
panicky that the sleep thing just ain't happening
for me tonight.

The worst thing you can do as an insomniac is
clock-watch, as you spend the entire night
calculating how little sleep you think you
might be getting. You reason that as long as

you fall asleep by 1 a.m. you'll be fine, as
that gives you six hours which is the minimum
you need to still be OK. The problem with this
is that you inevitably won't be able to fall
asleep by 1 a.m. and you then spend the rest
of the night worrying that you are now at a
critical level.

I start trying to tell my brain that I think we'll
be OK tomorrow if we get five and a half hours,
then five hours, then four and a half . . .

Sometimes I find myself and my brain have reached
stalemate at 3 a.m.

What I know about 3 a.m. is that it's the loneliest time of all. Too late to pretend you could still be up watching TV, too soon for even the earliest risers to be getting ready for work. The late-night cabs dropping people home from their nights out have stopped and the distant noise of milk floats or post vans is yet to break the silence.

At 3 a.m. it feels like you are the only one awake.

I can at this point feel so, so tired, even deliriously so, but my stupid stubborn brain still refuses to surrender to sleep.

Eventually, my brain usually gives in. On the worst occasions, though, it will keep me up all night. Sometimes it gives in and then wakes me up again two hours later, or – trickiest of all – it will let me fall asleep thirty minutes before I need to get up for the day! Thanks again, brain! Before I know it the sun is shining through the window, the kids are poking me in the eye and those bastard little tweety things are singing their goddamn morning chorus.

I have no choice but to crawl out of bed and face the day. The one thing that really helps is coffee. I can convince myself that everything will be OK if I can just have one little coffee. And it does help. The problem is that I really want more of its lovely warming goodness and coffee, although a temporary solution, is also part of the problem.

After a bad night's sleep, everything can seem impossible.

One time I was so tired on the way to work that I forgot I hadn't been to work yet and thought I was on the way home; other times I'm offering the kids a glass of wine before bed instead of milk, I'm looking for my phone whilst on the phone to somebody and then I'm throwing my phone in the bin.

I'm putting the car keys in the fridge and trying to unlock the car with the TV remote, I'm calling everyone in my family 'whatshisface' because I can't remember any of their names, next the floor has inexplicably turned into jam, the kids are velociraptors and my husband's head has morphed into a pan! Oh god, and I'm hallucinating again!

The list goes on. It becomes so very hard to think and function properly – no wonder sleep deprivation is a form of torture.

Once I have managed to get out and about I find that people like to helpfully inform me that I look a bit tired.

Except that because I have forgotten how to use words correctly, it will come out a bit more like . . .

And people will just think I have gone a bit mad. Which is accurate.

If I do manage to inform them that I look like death because I couldn't sleep, this will usually be met with helpful anecdotes about how easily they find it to nod off.

I have always envied the type of people who are able to fall asleep on demand – yes, you know who you are! I bet you'll be reading this chapter whilst smugly shaking your head thinking, 'Nope, not me, I can fall asleep on the toilet!'

Then they may start to offer up some trusty solutions.

Yes, I have tried meditating, yes, I have tried exercise, yes, I have tried spritzing my pillow with lavender, yes, I have tried every single drug I can get my hands on!

And yes, I have tried counting sheep but the little bastards are out to get me too!!

My insomnia certainly seems to have got worse
with age and particularly since having kids. Once
you become sleep-deprived at the hands of a small
person, you begin to value sleep more than ever.
In turn, placing more value on sleep leads you to
become more stressed about getting enough of it,
and getting stressed about sleep = no sleep. It's
a vicious cycle that you can't seem to fight your
way out of.

Recently, sleeping has become a little easier for
me. However, once insomnia has had you in her
grasp I don't think you can ever truly escape.
She is always there on the horizon, taunting you
and whispering threats. She still gives me the

occasional bad night, but the difference is that I have learned to give her the finger.

There are certain things that have helped:

- Finding out that I was not alone – insomnia is incredibly common.
- Knowing that it wasn't doing me any long-term harm or damage – some people learn to function just fine on very little sleep. Margaret Thatcher was famous for surviving on just four hours a night!
- On a practical level, focusing on my breathing or reciting song lyrics in my head helps to stop the negative thought cycle.
- Binning the sleeping pills. Though they did help, I would then feel even more anxious that I may only ever be able to sleep with the help of medication.
- Only going to bed when I was very tired and not napping in the day. I didn't want to get into a habit of sleeping at odd times, I just wanted to sleep at night.
- And mostly – knowing that if I could get through pan head, jam floor, velociraptor day . . . THEN I COULD GET THROUGH ANYTHING!!

CHRISTMAS IS NOT FOR ADULTS

They say that Christmas is for children and they're right, because it sure as hell isn't for adults.

I'm the type of person who would say 'I LOVE CHRISTMAS!' because on the face of it I do. All the things associated with Christmas I absolutely adore: carol singing, mulled wine, winter hats, log fires, fairy lights, festive films and family time. It's the time of year when it's perfectly acceptable to exist on a diet of Quality Street and Baileys. Seriously, what's not to like?

I'll tell you what the problem is: I never have time to enjoy ANY of those things because all of the pleasure is sucked out of Christmas by the huge amount of festive admin. My to-do list, which is horrific at the best of times, now goes into total overdrive and I struggle to stay afloat.

To do:
- Go to school Christmas concert.
- Go to school Christmas fair.
- Go to school Christmas play.

- Decide to live at school because easier.
- Realise can't actually attend school Christmas play because working.
- Explain to small child that Mummy can't attend first Christmas school play because of being a career-obsessed bitch.
- Cry a bit.
- Buy tub of Quality Street. Eat Quality Street whilst doing more crying.

- Organise Father Christmas visit?!?
- Choose school Christmas dinner options.
- Force children to write thirty pointless Christmas cards so we don't lose face.
- Buy jumper for school Christmas jumper day.
- Buy mince pies for various festive events.

- Buy own mince pies back at festive events.
- Wonder why I even eat mince pies when I don't really like them.
- Buy teachers large bottle of gin.
- Buy own self large bottle of gin.
- Buy ALL the things.
- Sponsor ALL the things.
- Bring in pound coins and randomly lob them around the playground whilst angrily singing 'It's the Most Wonderful Time of the Year'.

- Something about a Jesus fancy dress competition, or was that a hallucination?
- Bring in eyeballs on skewers for the PTA Christmas raffle.
- Donate kidney for school Christmas hamper.

- Remember to go to various friend/school/work fun festive socials.
- Remember to be a fun festive person at fun festive socials.
- Do all of the Christmas shopping.
- Do everything else as well.

By the time we actually limp towards the finish line that is Christmas Eve I am absolutely exhausted. The fantasy of sitting on the sofa watching a lovely Christmas movie with yummy M&S oven snacks goes out the window as I've never managed to get my wrapping done on time.

Christmas Eve imagined . . .

Ahh, feeling so festive and Christmassy!

Christmas Eve reality . . .

I finally stumble into bed in the early hours, only just remembering to gnaw at Rudolph's carrot and have a slug of FC's G&T. Actually TBF that's normally long gone.

I feel I could sleep for days, which is unfortunate as this is basically how our Christmas pans out . . .

3–5 a.m. Children come into room every thirty minutes asking, 'HAS HE BEEN?!'

5.05 a.m. Get up after approximately three hours of broken sleep and try to concentrate really hard on not being sick due to tiredness. Unfortunately it's not possible to adopt the usual technique of putting cartoons on and ignoring the kids because Christmas guilt requires that you be a willing participant in stocking-opening.

6.15 a.m. Stuff face with handfuls of chocolate coins for energy.

6.30 a.m. Caffeination – I don't know if it's a word but it should be.

7 a.m. onwards Continue stuffing face with chocolate coins and downing coffee until someone (not me, because *Daily Mail* readers already think I am an offensive alcoholic) suggests it would be a good idea to crack open the Bucks Fizz.

10 a.m. Family arrive and assemble for official present-opening. Brace self, cross fingers and come armed with screwdriver and batteries.

10.30 a.m. Hunt for survivors in the wreckage.

11 a.m. Lunch prep. I am the sous chef in our house and I take that role VERY seriously.

12.30 p.m. Some people go to the pub for a pint. Try and be in that group. The sous chef in particular could do with a break.

2 p.m. Lunch is ready!

2.02 p.m. Everyone sits down to enjoy a large, leisurely feast.

2.04 p.m. The children have finished eating.

2.06 p.m. The children are fighting.

2.46 p.m. The children are STILL fighting.

3 p.m. Right, that's it. I get that Christmas is for kids but they've had their fun, it was magical and all, but the magic is now looking a bit thin on the ground. Come to think of it, the magic has well and truly left the fucking building. There is only one thing for it, chuck gold coins at the small people and insist they keep at least one metre away from all adult humans.

4 p.m. YAY cocktail time! Make each round with decreasing skill and increasing alcohol.

5 p.m. Your intellectual level has now been reduced to that of a five-year-old. Adults are boring. Hang out with the kids again.

8 p.m. Try and wrestle the small people into bed and then watch depressing soaps, put the world to rights, argue about politics, eat oven snacks, do some angry washing-up and wander around carrying a pyramid of Ferrero Rochers whilst encouraging guests to role-play the Ambassador's Reception (note: if they refuse, they should not be invited into your home again).

11.37 p.m. Fall asleep in front of the TV with a breaded mozzarella stick stuck to your face and your hand submerged in a tub of Quality Street.

You is beautiful. You is amazing. You is the winner of Christmas!

Now in contrast, the period between Boxing Day and New Year's Eve is MUCH better. I never understand people who take their trees down on Boxing Day as that is when the fun really starts for me. It's the point when I begin to relax and enjoy myself because it becomes perfectly acceptable to sit about looking tired and unenthusiastic whilst shovelling huge amounts of food into your face, and no one really judges you for it.

The rules/etiquette/diets that we adhere to in normal life no longer apply. Everyone just kind of does whatever the hell they like for a few days – meandering from fridge to sofa to pub and so on, whilst feeling confused. No wonder they call it Chrimbo Limbo.

Unlike Roy Wood, I don't wish it could be Christmas every day, but I wouldn't mind being stuck in some sort of groundhog Chrimbo Limbo loop.

By the time it gets to January, normal life must resume again and it's always terribly sad and hard to accept.

January absolutely sucks arse because all anyone can talk about is their fucking diet/detox/ no-booze plans. Which is extra super bad if your birthday is in January like mine.

I'm not sure what's worse: the fact everyone has gone all clean living, or the fact that they won't stop banging on about it. I personally think it's the latter. Each to their own and all that, but if you get sick of people asking if you're doing dry January, then please feel free to cut this out and stick it on your forehead. Just remember to get it laminated first as it'll inevitably be pissing down/snowing/hailing out there.

Cut out and keep!

Reasons I'm not doing dry January:

1. Don't want to.
2. Like wine and don't wish to appear disloyal.
3. January already a miserable fucking bastard.
4. Just not going to do it, OK!
5. Fuck off.

THE 5K TO COUCH

For people who start off enthusiastically,
but are ultimately lazy bastards

FUNCTIONAL FIT HUMAN

Every couple of years I decide that I will become a person who exercises. I don't mean to spoil it for you but it never ends well.

It does start well, though. It starts with me enthusiastically joining the gym and buying new trainers, a water bottle and co-ordinating leisure-wear. I also get one of those iPhone holders for my arm to show how SERIOUS I am.

Hurrah – I look like a person who exercises and it immediately makes me feel fitter!

Ha, look at me being all fit like a functional human!

ALL THE GEAR AND NO IDEA

I really enjoy strutting around in my new leisure-wear. I sometimes wear it even if I'm not planning on going to the gym in the hope that having it on will inspire me to accidentally do some exercise. I especially like to wear it on the school run, where lots of people will see me. I don't even need to tell people that I go to the gym – my accessories are screaming it in their lazy-arse, non-gym-going faces.

It doesn't matter that I wish I was Sharon because I love sausage rolls and *Homes Under the Hammer*; what matters is that I am now a serious gym-goer who LOVES to exercise!

To make this extra super clear to everyone, I buy a yoga mat – the ultimate accessory! Then I dig out my NutriBullet and start making kale- and kiwi-based concoctions that look like pond slime. I carry them around in a flask because if someone doesn't see you drinking your horrendous homemade smoothie – is there any point in actually drinking it?

LOOK AT ME NOW, LOSERS!

My enthusiasm is sky high. This isn't a fad . . . oh no. This is a lifestyle choice and I'm loving it.

The problems only start when I realise that once I arrive at the gym I may have to do some actual exercise and the problem with the actual exercise is I don't really like it.

Reasons I don't like it include:
1. It's tiring.
2. It's too long/boring/hard.
3. I don't want to get all sweaty and disgusting.
4. Being sweaty and disgusting doesn't make me look fresh and serene like people on Instagram.
5. I'm unable to co-ordinate my limbs to the requirements of class routines. (I barely know my left or right. I still have to write with an imaginary pen to work out which hand is which.)
6. Essentially I can't be fucked.

So I enjoy the idea of being fit and I like looking like someone who is fit, but I don't want to have to put any effort in. It's very difficult to accept this; I want to be someone who wants to exercise but I'm not.

HOWEVER, I have made a serious commitment to myself to be a gym person and I cannot give up (yet). I cannot bear to think that Sharon will be proved right.

I decide to go to the gym three times a week, since that's a figure that sounds impressive to lazy, non-exercising bastards like my previous self.

Sometimes I go four times and then tell EVERYONE so that they know just how goddamn committed I am.

Things start to go downhill when after several (one) weeks of solid, hardcore exercise, I don't notice any difference. After all the effort I was making, buying all the stuff and doing all the exercise, I should surely now have a really tight cellulite-free butt. Strangely, it looks exactly the same. This throws me into a quandary.

All this time and effort and ... nothing?!
WHERE ARE THE MUSCLES?!

People tell me that going to the gym isn't really about making yourself look better, it's about taking care of your body so that you are healthier and will live longer. But I don't want to live longer – I just want to have arms like Jennifer Aniston!

I change my screensaver to a picture of Jennifer Aniston's arms and keep going to the gym.

Persevere. Persevere. Persevere.

Oh no. Now another problem. My knees start complaining.

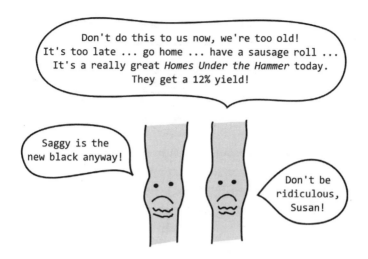

Also my back gets extremely fucked off.

So basically I exercised too hard and my body said 'No way'. Well, it's a good excuse and I'm sticking to it. Now I can tell people I can't go to the gym because of a sporting injury caused by excessive exercise, which makes me sound super extra fit.

When my knees are healed I know for sure that I'll go back to the gym. In fact, I can't wait! It's just a shame it's taking quite a long time.

Finally, two months later I'm fighting fit but I'm also extra busy with life/work/the kids so it's hard to fit the gym into my schedule. Maybe I'll cancel my membership for the time being and re-join when life is a little less hectic.

It's so hard to quit gyms, though – they always hit you with some really good logic.

Basically it's not worth cancelling because if I cancel and then re-join again (which I definitely will) then the price goes up by £5 a month and I'll lose my special introductory deal! So, being incredibly price-conscious, I keep paying the full membership even though I'm not going at all so that I can save £5 a month on the fees I would be paying if I quit and paid nothing and then signed up again later on.

Are you following? See, I told you - it's really great logic because I'm extra super definitely planning on going back to the gym next week . . . Or the week after . . .

Oh no, now a few more months have passed and I calculate that if I do start going, I will have to keep going for three more years until my logic actually does pay off. I'm more of a stop/starter so that's unlikely to happen. Dammit, I've been swizzled again.

But I can't let the gym think that they've won. OK, so I may look like the type of person that just pays gym membership for months on end without ever actually going, but that's just because I CHOOSE to go whenever I LIKE to. Which incidentally isn't very often.

SO in a feeble last-ditch attempt to show the gym that they're not the boss of me, I drag my sorry arse along to an ashtanga yoga class. But I don't enjoy it because after my sporting injury put me out of action for months, I'm not very fit; also I need to fart; and also, even though I'm trying really hard to be all mindful and zen, I can't help calculating what this class has actually cost me.

Gah.

Turns out I'm not destined to be one of those shiny, serene fitness gurus on Instagram who show off the bodies that they have worked hard to achieve. And, if they've been doing it healthily, why shouldn't they be proud?

There is now also a growing body positive movement, with women showing their bodies as they are - no angles; no filters; lumps, bumps, tummy folds and all. It's a truly great thing to be happy with what you've got and as long as they're doing it healthily, why shouldn't they be proud?

But sometimes I feel I'm stuck between a rock and a hard place, not fully able to identify with either end of the scale. Too lazy to have the perfect body and too vain to love my body as it is.

Then I remember that my body can be quite useful! It's here now typing words on a computer, it moves, it gets me from A to B, it can dance (badly) and run (a short distance for the bus). Although it could look better in swimwear (a lot better) it still puts swimwear on and dives into the sea on a hot day because I'm learning to not let it hold me back from enjoying life.

So maybe I'll never be a functional fit human, maybe I'll never be truly body confident, and maybe

I'll be stuck in a permanent state of 'I think I'm going to join a gym!' but at least I do have a body, at least there is *Homes Under the Hammer*, and at least I'll always have Sharon . . .

THINGS I ASPIRED TO WHEN I WAS YOUNGER...

A glittering career!

Hot boyfriend!

The perfect tan!!

Capsule collection wardrobe!

THINGS I ASPIRE TO NOW...

Bi-fold doors!

Kitchen island!

Cordless vacuum cleaner!

Utility room!

UNFORTUNATE SIGNS YOU
ARE GETTING OLDER

It happens to us all, this getting-older thing, and there is nothing you can do to fight it. One day you'll just be going about your business, being young and down with the kids when WHAM – what the hell?! You will realise that you are in fact in a completely different demographic age bracket to what you thought, and it's not just the wrinkles and aching body parts that give it away. You will start displaying lots of very worrying types of behaviour.

Why not take our 'Are you getting older?' quiz to see if you too fall into this category . . .

- Do you ever flick through a copy of *Heat* magazine and realise you know NO ONE in it?
- Do you wander around the house sighing for no particular reason?

- Are you considering signing up for a half-marathon?
- Do you enjoy working out ingenious ways to cheat the system with your Tesco Clubcard vouchers?

- Are you happy when it's a sunny day, mostly because you can dry the washing on the line?
- Do you complain that there is 'nothing good on the TV these days!'?
- Do you feel stupidly pleased with yourself for completing mundane tasks like finally ordering a new cutlery basket for the dishwasher?

- Would it ruin your ~~week~~ day if the new basket didn't fit properly?

- Would you panic if someone asked you to recommend a trendy bar in your local area? (FYI ones that shut down fifteen years ago don't count.)
- If you did have to go to a trendy bar would you basically pick the one most likely to have chairs?
- Do you feel elated when people cancel plans on you?

- Are 95% of the parties you get invited to kids' birthday parties (maybe even 99%)?
- On the rare occasions you do go out, do you behave like a total liability?
- Do you then wake up the next morning at 6 a.m. and have a hangover that lasts for three days?
- Have you started taking your slippers everywhere you go?

- When the toilet roll runs out, do you put a new roll straight on the holder instead of leaving it sitting on the floor?

- Do you count a trip to Homebase as a nice day out?
- When a younger person attempts to explain Snapchat to you, do you want to cry and shout 'MAKE IT STOP!'?
- Do you own any Le Creuset cookware?
- Is your metabolism shot to shit?
- Do you enjoy writing passive-aggressive emails to supermarkets?

```
To: Customer services
Subject: Mouldy grapes etc.

Dear Sir,

I am writing to inform you of my severe disappointment
concerning the purchase of one of your mixed grape punnets.
Having been an avid enjoyer for many years, I was surprised
to find said grapes soft, sour and somewhat mouldy!

I feel quite let down and sad if I'm honest ☹

FYI your 'fresh from the bakery' Rosemary & Sea Salt Focaccia
also felt firm to the touch within 24 hrs but I'm willing to
let that slide as a one-off incident.

Looking forward to hearing from you soon!

Kind regards from a loyal customer.

xxx
```

- Do you make multi-product purchases and store them in the cupboard like a hoarder instead of buying things as and when you need them?

- Have you recently joined the National Trust?
- Have you worked out the actual cost per visit vs the price non-members pay?
- Do you feel smug about that?
- Do you often feel smug about stupid unimportant shit that no one else cares about?

If you have answered yes to ten or more of the above statements then, like me, you are probably teetering perilously close to middle age. This can be hard to accept. I still remember being in school and thinking everyone's mums seemed like another species – so old, so tired-looking, so boring!

But now that's me. And I was right because I am old and tired-looking and boring. But that's not such a bad thing!

Being young may have been more fun and exciting but it was also a time full of horrible insecurities and self-doubt. One of the best things about getting older, I have realised, is that I am much more confident and comfortable in my own (slightly sagging) skin.

I am not young, I am not cool and I will never be young and cool again – nor do I want to be. Man, that shit was exhausting! There is something so freeing about throwing your hands up in the air and declaring yourself out of the game.

But, like, in your head, yeh? Don't do it in public as people tend to look at you funny.

These days I don't have to wear tiny, impractical clothes that make me feel cold and uncomfortable and I don't have to wear massive heels that make my feet hurt. I don't have to worry about having permanently smooth legs, immaculate nails or an excellent thigh gap because I have none of those things and, really, who has the time and energy?

I don't have to try and impress people I don't really like and I don't have to spend days fretting over whether some idiot boy will text me back. I don't go to parties because I'm afraid of missing out, because I no longer care about missing out. Usually I welcome missing out.

Instead I have perspective. I have stories to tell. I have laughter lines because I laugh a lot. In fact, I have a growing list of imperfections but that's (mostly) fine because we all do and no one even fucking notices anyone else's.

I have wonderful family and friends, who despite all of my flaws and shortcomings (and maybe even because of them) love me anyway.

Most importantly I have a comfy sofa, a bowl of popcorn and a terrible movie to watch, and this is where you'll find me 90% of the time, because once I've put my bunny-rabbit slippers on I'm not going anywhere for anybody.

I know I'm lucky to be here and to have all that
I have, so I'm choosing to age gracefully like
a bottle of fine wine, or at least a moderately
priced Malbec.

After all, they say that life begins at forty,
don't they?

DON'T THEY?!

. . . it just seems a real shame that by then,
you're already halfway dead.

SMALL THINGS THAT MAKE ME HAPPY

A few weeks ago I was walking home from school with my kids and we saw a boy fall off his scooter and start crying. 'Oh dear, that poor boy,' I said. My eight-year-old turned to me and said, 'That boy kicked me the other day for no reason!'

'Oh, I see,' I said. 'Have you ever heard of karma?'

'No,' he said.

So I explained to him that sometimes when nasty things happen to good people, at some point later on the force of good – whether that be the universe, or God or whatever greater being you choose to believe in – will come along and right that wrong.

'Oh,' he said, 'so Jesus pushed that boy off his scooter?'

'Sort of,' I said.

The upshot was that neither of us felt very bad for the boy any more – justice had been done.

[FYI before you go thinking I'm a total bitch, he had just grazed his knees a bit and was fine.]

Anyway, it got me thinking . . . The world we live in can be pretty shitty, but there are also many lovely, good and happy moments mixed in with the shitty stuff. Sometimes you just have to press pause for a minute to truly appreciate them.

Here are a few of the small things that make me happy:
- The right bus arriving just as I get to the bus stop.
- Things turning out cheaper than I expected at the cash register.
- People who were mean to me at school ageing really badly.
- A horribly miserable rainy, dark day when I'm hungover.
- Blissful morning sun when I'm not.
- Breaking the seal.

- Watching *MasterChef* whilst eating fish fingers and beans for dinner with a glass of Pinot Noir.
- Or Coco Pops and rosé.
- Seeing other people in the street losing their shit at their children (and knowing that I'm not the only one).
- My dog, just being my dog.
- The satisfaction I get after hoovering under furniture for the first time in six months (two years).

- Being really nice to someone who is trying to argue with me – just to annoy them.
- Reading about the downfall of celebrities I don't like.
- Smelling someone else's perfume/aftershave and being transported right back to the middle of a memory from twenty years ago.
- Sticking my head in the fridge and having a good old swear.

- Going to bed early and actually being able to get to sleep.
- Finding an excellent parking spot and parking in it really well.
- Getting an answer that no one else knows in a quiz.
- The dog doing a really bad fart in public and laughing uncontrollably with the kids about it.
- Writing down things I've already done on my to-do list just to cross them off.
- Drinking white wine at a great restaurant outside in the sun, knowing everyone else is at work.
- Throwing something at a bin from far away and actually getting it in.
- Discovering a hidden Easter egg I'd forgotten about.
- Sneezing in a public place and a stranger saying, 'Bless you.'
- Waking up with clear skin on the day of an important event.
- Butterscotch Angel Delight.
- Finding a fiver in my back pocket.

- Cracking out a brand-new washing-up sponge.

- Making ludicrous, unachievable plans for the future even though I know they'll never happen.
- Every sock having its pair when I match them up after the wash.
- Going away for the weekend and having no plans but everything going right.
- Seamlessly quoting Alan Partridge in relevant conversations.
- Being really thirsty, having a drink and saying 'Ahhhhhhh!'
- Being desperate for the loo, having a wee and saying 'Ahhhhhhh!'
- A satisfying poo.

- Place and street names that sound rude.

- Selling stuff I was going to throw away and then feeling like I got free money.
- Telling a really good story to avid listeners.
- Clouds that look like private parts.
- Taking someone down a peg or two (in my head).
- Trying to choose between two equal-length queues at the supermarket and correctly picking the one that moves the quickest.
- Making decisions and not even bothering to justify them to other people.
- The smell of cut grass.
- A good old bitch.
- When the whole family is really kind and nice to each other all day (or maybe just for fifteen minutes or so).

- Cooking pasta and getting the quantity EXACTLY right.

- Warming cold toes on a radiator.
- Feeling under pressure to do something I don't want to do and then not doing it and feeling, for once, in control of my life.
- Giving someone a compliment and realising how much it meant to them.
- When the shampoo and conditioner runs out at the same time.

- A deep bubble bath and a good book.
- Shaving my legs without cutting them.
- A day off, just to myself.
- Trying to decide between two options on a menu and when my meal arrives seeing that I made the right choice and someone else made the wrong choice and trying to keep my joy inside but failing, and everyone else trying to keep their envy inside but failing – and knowing that even if it was just for a moment, the universe was truly on my side.

- And finally, when I'm feeling a little bit down, I think about Jesus going around pushing little kids off scooters and that always cheers me up. Try it!

THE END.

ACKNOWLEDGMENTS

You're a
total gem!

Firstly a big thank you to my lovely followers and readers who continue to support me even when I keep going AWOL!

To my editor Hannah for being so supportive and wonderful to work with, to Emma – it's always a delight and to Jasmine, Fiona, Alice and everyone at Hodder for everything you do.

To Charlotte for kicking this all off, I hope this version is a tiny bit less ranty!

To Amber for being a kick-ass copy editor and making me smile with all of your notes.

To Jon and Millie for being excellent at the agency stuff.

To all of my (too many to mention) family and friends for being you.

To Sasha AKA 'Second Place' for being the best dog with the best hair.

To all three of my boys, because I'd much rather be overwhelmed than underwhelmed.

Lastly thank you to me, because I wrote the bloody thing!

ABOUT THE AUTHOR

Katie is a human being who lives by the sea in Hove with her family.

She used to have a proper professional job but now she just draws pictures of sweary stick people which she much prefers.

She hates camping but enjoys drinking wine out of plastic mugs. Grumpy Bear was her favourite Care Bear.

hurrahforgin.com
facebook.com/hurrahforgin
Instagram and Twitter - @hurrahforgin